THE BEST OF
AMERICAN GARDENING

Other Kraft Books

Grow Your Own Dwarf Fruit Trees
Growing Food the Natural Way
The Home Garden Cookbook
Fruits for the Home Garden
Luther Burbank, the Wizard and the Man
Rainbow by the Bayou
Gardener, Go Home
Garden to Order
Give Father a Hard Knock
The Birds and the Beasts Were There
Land of Milk and Omelets

The Best of
AMERICAN
GARDENING
Two Centuries of Fertile Ideas

Ken and Pat Kraft

WALKER AND COMPANY
NEW YORK

First published in the United States of America
in 1975 by the Walker Publishing Company, Inc.

Published simultaneously in Canada by
Fitzhenry & Whiteside, Limited, Toronto.

ISBN: 0-8027-0497-2

Library of Congress Catalog Card Number: 75-9307

Printed in the United States of America.

Book Design by Amy Bisso.

10 9 8 7 6 5 4 3 2 1

THIS BOOK is for our friends Gordon and Sassy—
Mr. and Mrs. Gordon Baker Lloyd, who have done so
much to help gardeners enjoy their gardens.

ACKNOWLEDGMENTS We are grateful to many for help with this book, so many that a complete listing of their names is now impossible. We do wish, however, to take this opportunity of thanking: Frederick E. Bauer, Jr., of the American Antiquarian Society; David Burpee, Jerome H. Kantor, and Miss Jeannette Lowe of W. Atlee Burpee Company; Ms Jocelyn E. Granet of Ferry Morse Seed Company; Miss Beatrice F. Howitt; Miss Barbara Lowenstein; Robert H. Land of the Library of Congress; William J. Park of George W. Park Seed Company; the Port Townsend, Washington, Public Library staff and especially Librarian Mrs. Charles E. Wallin; Kenneth Relyea of Farmer Seed & Nursery Company; Miss Rachel Snyder of Flower and Garden Magazine; the University of California, Davis, Library staff, with particular gratitude to Mrs. Helen Fontes, Assistant Curator, F. Hal Higgins Library of Agricultural Technology; and Charles B. Wilson of Joseph Harris Company.

Our appreciation is due the following for making available to us the authentic old illustrations used in this book: W. Atlee Burpee Company; Don Kunitz, Department of Special Collections, University Library, University of California, Davis, California; Geo. W. Park Seed Company; Gordon Baker Lloyd; The Mount Vernon Ladies' Association of the Union; and National Agricultural Library.

CONTENTS

Two Centuries of Advise
to the Home Gardener

OUR aim in writing this book has been to discover how American home gardeners were coping with their problems, enjoying their gardens, and living better because of them, during the past two centuries. In some cases we went back farther, as an era limitation is sometimes artificial, and also, the earliest American gardening skill was imported from still earlier times in the Old World.

In telling of yesterday's gardening methods and materials we have tried to screen out those that seem to lack practical worth today, no matter how interesting they may be. Where there was a reasonable doubt we included the old way.

The result, we hope, will open to the gardener-reader a door to gardening knowledge of the past, an often sophisticated and highly effective knowledge that richly deserves rediscovery.

Along with what they found out on their own as to gardening conditions in the New World, American gardeners of the 18th and 19th centuries had plenty of advice given them by the printed word. Sometimes stern, often lively, it appeared in books, periodicals, and seed catalogs.

The books frequently took the forms of almanacs and agricultural dictionaries, a pattern set in England. The first to appear in America was Samuel Dean's *The New-England Farmer or Georgical Dictionary*, a book of more than 300 pages, first published in 1790 by Isaiah Thomas at Worcester, Massachusetts. It was followed by several others, including some American editions of English works. The alphabetical form was the usual early makeup, and most such books went into several editions. Henry Ward Beecher took time out in the 1840s from preaching and abolitionist activities to write articles on gardening, later collected in a book called *Plain and Pleasant Talk about Fruits, Flowers, and Farming*. After the midpoint of the 19th century there was a rash of specialty books, as on composting, vegetable gardening, coping with pests, running a hotbed, and so on.

The periodicals flourished greatly in the 19th century, and a good deal of farming and gardening information also appeared in general magazines and newspapers. Among specialized magazines were *The Rural American, The American Farmer, The Cultivator, The New England Farmer, The Southern Agriculturist, The Farmer's Register, Western Farmer and Gardener, Hovey's Magazine of Horticulture, Scientific Farmer, Gardener's Monthly and Horticulturist*, and *Park's Floral Magazine* (originally *Gazette*), this last said to be the first one addressed to the home flower growers.

There was an intimate feeling about the old gardening magazines. Readers often seemed to feel themselves banded together in a clubby intimacy. This was sometimes shown in items that appeared in what were called exchange columns. Thus, in the Park magazine, an Illinois lady rashly addressed her sister gardeners of the entire United States with: "I will exchange anything I have to spare for slips of the fuchsias Sunrise and Sunray."

Other exchange items:

"Frank C. Smith of New York City has pieces of calico and

satin suitable for patchwork, to exchange for plants, bulbs, or seeds."

"Would like, in exchange specimens for a loose parlor cabinet. Will exchange plants in the spring."

"Mattie Burch of Oakville, Washington Territory, will exchange knitting pattern of laces, mittens, or hoods for flower seeds, bulbs, &c. Instructions for knitting sent with each pattern if desired."

"Mrs. S.W. Phipps, Charlemont, Mass., wishes to give lessons in painting (by mail) in exchange for flower seeds or bulbs."

"Miss P.W. Wiley, Danvers Centre, Massachusetts, would like to exchange a receipt to make nice perfumery for seeds, bulbs, etc."

By the time the 19th century was well along, the seed catalogs were becoming very informative references for gardeners, as most of them are today. This advice from the Germain Fruit Company's 1896 catalog and from the 1881 D.M. Ferry & Company one is typical:

"Do not attempt too much."

"Cultivate deeply, viz.: from 15 to 20 inches."

"Keep weeds down. The old adage, 'One year's seeding makes seven years' weeding' is correct."

"Care should be taken that the productiveness of the garden be not diminished by the proximity of large trees which are injurious by their drip to all plants beneath them and by their shade and extended roots to those more remote."

"The surface of the soil cannot be too frequently stirred . . . if the ground be suffered to become close and compact, the cool surface exposed to the air for the reception of moisture is smaller, and what is deposited does not enter into the earth far enough to be appropriated."

In addition to giving advice, the old seedsmen sometimes sought it, so that years ago the customers helped with the testing of some novelties and occasionally named them as well. In 1883 the W. Atlee Burpee company sent free packets of a likely looking new lettuce to a few hundred customers to try out under various local growing conditions. It was designated Sample No. 33, and a gardener in Connecticut waxed lyrical in his report— "Large, handsome, firm . . ."—and was so carried away by the lettuce's appealing center he suggested it be called Golden Heart, which it promptly was.

Following is some of the more specific gardening counsel handed out on some areas of broad garden interest. The listing is alphabetical, under the headings: Cultivation, Fencing, Hand Care, Hotbeds, Magnetism, Moon Influence, Mulching, Rotation, Seeding, Tools, Transplanting, Watering, and Weeding.

CULTIVATION

In earlier times, thorough and repeated digging and cultivation of garden soil was standard practice, almost gospel. Seedsman D.M. Ferry warned his customers in 1911: "Rich soil and liberal manuring will avail little without thorough preparation. The soil must be made friable by thorough and judicious working." Sixty years before this, in 1851, Cuthbert William Johnson was telling readers of the American edition of his *Farmer's Enclycopaedia and Dictionary of Rural Affairs:* "The operation of hoeing is destructive of weeds and renders the soil more permeable to the gases and aqueous vapor of the atmosphere . . . This appears by the plants which flourish, whilst those in hard ground are starved. In the driest weather good hoeing procures moisture to the roots of plants, though the ignorant and incurious fancy it lets in the drought."

This approach has been modified today by many gardeners so that some never turn the soil, and others only to work organic matter into the upper few inches, a permanent mulch being relied on to keep the earth in a productive state.

The minimum-tillage gardeners had their viewpoint bol-

4

stered by an experiment of University of California agronomists in 1971-73 on wheat and barley. They found yields were not helped by an extra disking before seeding, although it produced a much smoother looking seed bed.

Designs for woven garden fences, made of slender tree branches. The bark was not removed.

FENCING

Here is advice from 1790 by Samuel Deane on fencing a garden: "PALE, a pointed stake used in making enclosures, partitions, and so forth. Gardeners oftentimes have occasion to make pale fences to secure choice apartments from the entrance of tame fowls, which will not often fly over a paled or picketed fence: As well as to prevent the intrusion of idle and mischievous people."

Some 30 years later, William Cobbett, an Englishman writing in America about American gardens, was urging the planting of hawthorn hedges around gardens in the English manner, for protection against intruders, for shelter as a windbreak, and for shade in hot weather.

HAND CARE

A recipe for a gardener's hand cream, circa 1886: "At night, rub on the hands a little lard and white wax melted together, or mutton tallow." (See Chapter 7 for other skin care products.)

HOTBEDS

The hotbed, to protect tender plants from cold weather and to help sprout seeds has been used for centuries. Manure usually supplied the heat, and a vegetable compost will do it for a shorter time. Today electric cables can serve the purpose. The rationale of a hotbed for starting plants ahead of time was given by Cobbett in 1821 when he wrote: "Hotbeds are more necessary in America because the winter will not suffer to exist in the open air many plants which are wanted to start with the warm sun. . . . There is no spring, but a sudden transition from winter to summer which presents the gardener with a sun ready to push forward every plant, but alas, he has no plants."

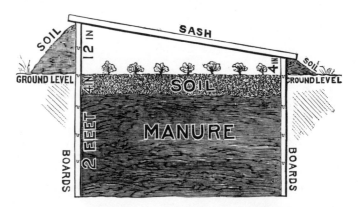

Cross section of a hotbed with a 2' layer of fermenting stable manure below for heat. Plants are growing in 4" of soil on top —or can be grown in flats set on the manure. The sash on top is slanted to shed water, and soil is banked around the frame for protection from cold. If the manure is omitted, the structure is a cold frame.

A simple explanation of a hotbed, from an old seed catalog, ran: "Simply a boarded-up garden covered with glass." Glass was not always used, though. "Those who are too poor to afford sash of glass," an 1880 gardener observed, "use muslin covers for hotbeds. I am using them and find them just the thing. I am often away from home at the time it is necessary to attend to glass, and yet my plants have not suffered." He was referring to the need for ventilation of the hotbed.

Here is some typical advice given 19th century gardeners on setting up a hotbed:

> Fresh stable manure in which there is plenty of litter is most suited for hotbeds. There should be at least one-third litter in the heap. Shape it up well and mix it well together, adding water if at all dry and musty, and throw it into a compact heap to ferment. Let it remain a week and then work it over thoroughly as before, and water if necessary.
>
> On this place the frame, which should be smaller than the heap of manure. Get a lot of boxes about five or six inches high. Sow the seeds in these, and place them on the manure inside the frame; this is much better than to fill soil in the frame.
>
> Great care must be taken after the plants appear, to prevent them from becoming scorched or slender. During mild sunny days the heat inside the frame will be intense, and unless air be given freely the plants will wither and die. On the other hand there is often a spell of cold weather after the hotbed is set up, and when this prevails the frames should be sheltered with old carpet or mattresses so that the

Coldframe with straw mat laid over the sash for frost protection. Burlap or sheet plastic such as a shower curtain can do the same job.

A coldframe, showing a simple ventilating device—a notched stick for propping up the sash when weather permits. Although the illustration is old, the arrangement is still used.

A good and simple old way to protect young transplants from hot sun until they are established is by slanting a board over the row on the south side. Hold it in place with sticks pushed into the ground.

soil inside may not become cold and thus cause the seeds to rot or the plants to die. As the season advances and the rays of the sun become more genial, give the glass one or two coats of whitewash.

Another coating used was one part of linseed oil to five parts of turpentine, brushed on lightly.

A coldframe is a hotbed without an interior source of warmth. It depends on the sun for heat. It offers enough protection, however, to keep some half-hardy plants alive in winter, and to give tender ones a head start in spring.

MAGNETISM

In 1877 an experienced New York State gardener reported on this experiment to stimulate growth of a tea rose with what he called electricity and which has also been called magnetism. "I went to a tinsmith and directed him to cut a strip of sheet copper," the gardener related, "three-quarters of an inch wide and 15 inches long—also one of sheet zinc of the same size. One end of the zinc was fastened to the copper with a small rivet. They made a strip 29 inches long, which I bent over the plant in the shape of a horseshoe, and stuck the two ends well down into the earth on each side of the plant, the earth between them completing the circuit. In three weeks the plant had more than half doubled its original size, and is still growing like Jack's bean stalk. I am now experimenting on other plants with good results. I set them in short rows, and bend the electrical strips from one end of the rows to the other. I am also trying it in pots with good results. After the plants get a good start I take the strips away."

We ran across another magnetism item, recounted by Henry Ward Beecher in the 1840s. Quoting a contemporary farmer on planting potatoes, he said they should be placed so as "to point north and south."

MOON INFLUENCE This planting-by-the-moon advice was passed along to readers of *Park's Floral Magazine* in the fall of 1886 by a gardener in Maryland:

"I used to laugh at persons sowing seeds in the different signs but experience has taught me better. One of my neighbors planted her garden peas this spring in the sign of the Virgin, consequently they have done nothing but blossom, and now I am very sorry I did not plant my sweet 'flowering peas' in the same sign. But I always try to make it suit to sow my flower seeds in that sign and just before the full moon. You will be amply repaid, especially with single varieties that you must save seeds from, such as petunias, ten-week stock, daisies, and so forth. Last November I planted my tulips in the increase of the moon and planted them very deep, too, but they nearly all came to the surface. I will not have to dig for them, for I can pull them up without any trouble."

Another gardener answered shortly after: "I am not at all superstitious in regard to the moon; but I know from long experience that planting seed of single flowers just before the full moon will insure more double flowers than if sown otherwise. The moon certainly has an influence upon plants. I know that if the yucca Filimentosa does not bloom just about the full moon it will not bloom at all."

Another gardener was even more emphatic as to double

9

flowers: "In my opinion the time of sowing has much to do with the duplicity of the flowers. I plant my seeds when the moon is full and get double flowers every time. I save good seed from double flowers."

And: "Sow your fall turnips," an 18th-century farmer advised, about midsummer, and "if about the full moon, the better," although the dark of the moon usually was thought the proper timing for root crops.

MULCHING

In former days, clean cultivation was far more practiced than was mulching. When mulching was done, the purpose was most apt to be for protection from cold. An exception to this was the mulching of potatoes described by Isaiah Thomas in 1790 (quoted in Chapter 4).

In the 1870s the New York *Tribune* gave this simple but often misunderstood reason for a straw or other mulching protection of half-hardy plants in winter: "Don't kill with kindness; don't give a mulch of manure that would cover the garden and then expect the poor plant to survive. This is almost certain death. The object is not to keep the plant warm, but to preserve it cool and free from the fluctuating temperatures of our trying winter. Sudden freezing and thawing is what does the mischief."

ROTATION

Some 1896 advice on rotation of garden crops ran: "Attend strictly to rotation of crops. Do not let two tap-rooted crops (as carrots and parsnips) follow each other, nor two exhaustive head crops (as cabbages and cauliflowers). Let the soil have time to recuperate its exhausted fertility. Follow carrots, for instance, with a surface, shallow feeding crop, as peas, or vine crops, as melons and squashes." We might add that although peas are light feeders, the vine crops are not—but rotation is a good idea for other reasons just the same.

In 1851 Johnson said: "It is known to every cultivator of soil that land soon becomes tired of the same crop; in many instances, peculiar diseases are induced by the repetition. The most beneficial plan of rotation appears to be that where an exhausting and non-exhausting crop alternately succeed each other, for example: Onions, lettuce, carrots, manure; [or] turnips, peas, potatoes, manure." The manure rotation here could be a green-manure crop such as rye or clover, to be turned under, or a dressing of stable manure. Another rotation suggested by Johnson for poor land was celery, cauliflower with beets, onions, and peas.

SEEDING

To sprout, seeds need moisture, oxygen, and warmth. Some seeds —lettuce, spinach, and peas are three—will sprout in soil as cool as 40° F., but most need a temperature of 70° F., or higher. A good old-fashioned way to hold the sun's warmth in the soil for sprouting seeds is this one, given for corn but good for other crops: If the earth was spaded the previous fall, merely hoe and rake the surface before seeding, since the upper 6" of soil is much warmer than that below it.

In 1876 a Wisconsin gardener wrote her seedsman, Mr. George W. Park, her method of sprouting verbena seed. "An old pan of soil (well heated in the stove oven, to kill any weed seeds or insect eggs that may be in it) may be sowed with verbena seed the last of February, or first of March, set back of a stove that is used constantly, so as to keep it continually warm, and covered closely with thick cloth to keep the moisture in the soil . . . cover more closely at night, to retain all the heat possible." A warm place near a furnace duct can be substituted for the wood stove, and the method will work with other slow-germinating seeds, such as parsley. A sheet of plastic wrap stretched over the soil container will keep moisture in the soil better than a cloth, with no added moisture needed until sprouts appear and the plastic is removed.

Another 19th-century Wisconsin gardener advised this way of sprouting extremely small seeds: Fill a clay pot with a very fine soil mixture, sprinkle seeds on soil surface without covering them, place a sheet of glass over the pot and put the pot in a pan of water. "The water will draw up to the surface" of the soil.

Another old technique for sprouting tiny seeds, or even fern spores, was: "Get a soft brick, hollow out one of its sides, place some sifted woods earth in the cavity, press it down smooth, and sow the seeds over the surface. Now set the brick in a pan of water in a shady place. When the little plants get large enough they can be transplanted into pots of soil." In this method the seeds are not covered at all.

Seeding in eggshells was often done years ago, and is still a good technique to know about. Here is the method, as described in 1880 by an experienced gardener: "Take eggshells cut in half, make two or three small holes in bottom of each, fill with sifted soil, sink in a box of sand, sow seeds and cover with glass, of course keeping them in the right light. Water only the sand, for they will absorb enough through the holes in the shells. In transplanting, all you have to do is break off the shells, leaving the lump of earth intact without the roots being jarred or disturbed."

Here's a hint from the 19th century for germinating hard-coated seeds: "Procure a box 6 inches deep, put in 2 inches of broken crock pieces, then three inches of fine, porous soil. Plant the seeds in the soil and cover with an inch of finely chopped moss. Sink the box in the garden in a shady spot to keep it moist until seeds germinate. Sow only one kind of plant per box, as germination times differ." Some seeds treated in this way were cyclamen, smilax, violets, gentians, cannas, Christmas roses, and nasturtiums.

TOOLS

Most of the gardening jobs we do today had to be done a century or two ago, and the hand tools used for them had been well thought out by then. But there was more variety within classes of

These garden tools date back several centuries, having been ancient even in 1725 when they were shown in Richard Bradley's Survey *of Ancient Husbandry and Gardening. But their forms had not changed much by American colonial times, and nearly all are in use today in basically the same general designs.*

the old tools, almost as if every gardener had his own idea of what a spade or a weeder ought to look like—and, to be sure, a good many such tools were made by the gardeners who used them.

Basic garden tools were described in Deane's book previously

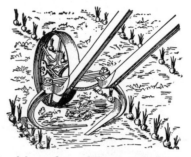

Wheel hoe, for cultivating and weeding.

mentioned. Hoes were in constant use, of course, narrow ones being employed for cultivating, and broad ones for breaking clods. Another hoe of sorts came into use later, perhaps for gentlemen gardeners, it being a kind of walking stick with a 2"-wide chisel blade on the end; called a spud, it was to cut weeds as one walked the garden grounds. Deane described what he called a prong-hoe; if it had two prong-like blades it was called a bidens (a tool that dated back to ancient Rome), and if three, a trident: "It is easily struck into the ground; and as the tines are six or seven inches long, it will stir the ground to the same depth that a plough does. It is useful in taking up strong-rooted weeds, and opening land that is crusted, or become too compact."

A hoe with the curious name of zapetino sounds like something known today: "This instrument is a small hoe at one end and has two prongs at the other. It is sometimes made with an eye for the insertion of the handle; sometimes with a shank to drive into the handle. With one end of this instrument, weeds are cut up in gardens; with the other, roots are drawn out and the ground loosened to the depth of five or six inches."

The dibble was described as a stick to make a hole to set a plant, and was sometimes tipped with metal.

Wheelbarrows, often homemade and with a wooden wheel, were in constant use.

Ploughs were also in general use and were termed by Deane "the most important of all the tools used in husbandry."

Digging tools included crowbars, then called crows; mattocks; and spades. For digging drain-tile lines, spades were made in a variety of specialized shapes, including triangular and sugar-scoop.

The rake was a well-known tool to early American gardeners, as it was to English ones and others. Wooden rakes were common, but metal kinds were used too, as shown in this description of spring-tooth rakes in John Monk's *Agricultural Dictionary* of 1794, an English book. "These rakes are in high repute; and it is the general opinion that one person will do more with this rake than four with the common wood rake . . . by the lower class of people they are called hell-rakes, on account of the great quantity of work they dispatch in a short time. . . . The teeth screw in and are fastened with screw-nuts."

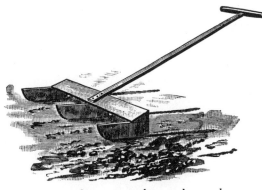

Home-made row marker—the push type.

When the wheel-hoe and allied tools appeared on the garden scene in the 19th century, the appeal of machinery to the average American probably did as much to make the new tools quickly popular as did their speed and efficiency. One enamoured gardener wrote to the manufacturer of his Planet Jr. item, in 1914: "I have used one of your seeders for about 25 years past,

15

but it has finally met an accident by misuse—got broken—and I am in a mess for fair to do by hand what it does so easily." Another said of an $11 combined seeder, wheel hoe, cultivator, and plough: "You can't buy mine for $100 and have me without one." A third man remarked of his wheel hoe: "Why, my 5-year-old boy could push it anywhere," but a smoother customer reported: "My wife can use it as well as I."

TRANSPLANTING

The introduction of the peat seeding block has simplified transplanting today. Seeds are planted in the blocks and when the resulting plants are moved to the garden, the blocks go too. The result is, the plants hardly know they have been moved, and suffer no transplanting shock. The eggshell seeding described previously was an early version of the peat block, and so was this sensible little strategy suggested in the 1890s but known for years before that: "A safe plan is to sow about five seeds on reversed pieces of sod about 4 inches square. On planting in the ground, insert the sod with the growing plants, and firm the soil in the usual way." In those days, transplanting was also called "after-planting."

"Transplanting," ran old advice, "is most apt to be successful if done just at evening, or immediately before or during the first part of a rain, about the worst time being just after a rain, when the ground being wet, it is impossible to sufficiently press it about the plant without its baking hard."

Another bit of old advice ran: "If there is not as much soil on the roots as you desire, make a 'puddle' of thick muddy water in a pail, wash-tub, or half-barrel, get a handful of plants and dip the roots in this muddy water."

The old seedsman Joseph Harris offered this tart comment on the custom of yanking at plants after transplanting, to see if they were set firmly: "A man may press the soil so firmly around the stem, the plant would stand quite a pull while in fact there might be a hollow space about the roots. This is like leaving your feet bare and trying to keep them warm by putting on a pair of garters." The proper way, of course, is to press soil well about the roots and then to water thoroughly.

"A good way to revive newly set, drooping plants," went some more old advice, "is to place a flower pot close to the plant, press it down in the earth, and fill it with water, which will gradually filter through the hole in the bottom and moisten the ground at the roots of the plant."

This heroic advice on transplanting things that are ordinarily hard to transplant came from an Indiana gardener in 1879: Such plants, she said, can "be taken up in the winter when the ground is frozen hard, by digging up a clump of earth with an axe, and the plant put where it is wanted to grow. It will awaken in the spring and not know the change."

WATERING

An experienced nurseryman gave this method, in 1878, of deep-watering garden plants. Beside each at the time of planting he sank a piece of 4" drain tile as deeply as the plant's roots reached, resting the bottom end of the tile on a brick or flat rock, and covering its top end, reaching slightly above ground level, with a rock. He found that filling the tile with water twice a week was often enough, and he added fertilizer to the water when needed. For larger plants he used a 6" tile. A length of old downspout would serve the same purpose as a tile.

The case for tepid water was stated in an old gardening magazine: "Where a vigorous growth of foliage is desired, or if we should wish to increase the size of the flowers, it is always an advantage to use warm water, instead of that direct from the well or cistern. Water may be warmed for this purpose by allowing it to stand in vessels or tubs exposed to the sun during the heat of the day." Today a metal drum in the garden, kept filled with rainwater from a downspout if possible, can furnish tepid water, and a few plants growing around it will provide a suitable screen for appearances' sake.

The old belief in rainwater as the proper water for plants has some modern scientific reinforcement. At the Agricultural Research center in Apopka, Florida, it was found that faucet water containing even minute amounts of fluoride caused tipburn and spotting of the leaves of some plants. These happened to be ornamental plants, but this does not rule out the chance of injury to some others. The study also found small amounts of fluorine present in perlite and in sphagnum moss.

WEEDING

By far the most weeding was done years ago with some of the tools mentioned earlier, and hoeing was an art. But gardeners are always looking for easier ways, and here are some that were tried:

A vigorous approach was advocated by an 1890 gardener. After preparing the seed bed, he wrote, "the writer prefers to cover the surface with a moderately thick layer of dry straw which is then sprinkled with kerosene oil and burned. The intense heat produced will destroy the vitality of all weed seeds within an inch or two of the surface, and save much future labor. Then rake the bed with a fine steel rake until the soil is perfectly fine and level." Burning off brush or stubble already on the land was a frequent sanitation practice, the resulting ash also being valued as fertilizer, but the above is the only case we came across in which the material to be burned was brought to the garden.

"If fresh oak sawdust be scattered on gravel walks," reads advice from the 1840s, "it effectually prevents the growth of weeds."

Henry Ward Beecher recounted this approach, also during the 1840s: "The following method to destroy weeds is pursued at the mint in Paris, with good effect: 10 gallons of water, 20 lbs. quicklime and 2 lbs. flowers of sulphur are to be boiled in an iron vessel; after settling, the clear part is thrown off and used when needed. Care must be taken, for if it will destroy weeds it will just as certainly destroy edgings and border flowers if sprinkled on them. Weeds, thus treated, will disappear for several years."

CHAPTER

TWO

Old-Time Fertilizers, Good Today

THE variety of fertilizers once used was wonderful, and included many that have been lost sight of. They are covered in alphabetical order here, and we have paid the most attention to natural fertilizers. But this does not mean that factory-made fertilizers were not in existence more than a hundred years ago. Called artificial manures, these included various secret patented mixtures such as "Alexander's Compost" and "Trimmer's Composition," along with muriate of ammonia, nitrate of soda, soda ash, sulfate of iron, silicate of potash, and others.

The role of the three elements needed in most quantity, along with the role of lime, was well stated over fifty years ago in the Farmer Seed Company's catalog: "Nitrogen produces early, rapid, and succulent growth of plant. Potash hardens plant growth and throws the vigor into fruit or flower. Phosphoric acid aids in nutrition, influences maturity and color. Lime releases inert plant foods, rendering them available for feeding roots."

Standard advice some 80 years ago was, "Fertilize liberally

19

before plowing or harrowing." A century before that, the fertilizing was sometimes omitted between some crops, as it sometimes is today, in which case the old term used to describe the planted land was "soil simple."

AMMONIA

Household ammonia was a popular fertilizer for house plants in the last century. It is still good, as we have determined by use. Amounts varied, usually from one teaspoon to one tablespoon to a gallon of water, applied in place of the usual watering, about once a month. The fertilizing element in ammonia is nitrogen. This report on use of ammonia was made by a reader to a gardening periodical of the 1880s:

"I put four chrysanthemum plants by themselves and gave them a teaspoon of ammonia in a gallon of water twice a week. In a fortnight the result was most striking for though I watered the others with liquid cow manure they looked lean when compared with the ammonia-watered plants, whose leaves turned to a very dark green, which they carried to the edge of the pots until the flowers were out. As a matter of course the flowers were splendid. I also tried it on strawberries with the same satisfactory result, the crop being nearly double that of the others."

ASHES

Hardwood ashes are still used as a fertilizer, especially for root crops, and were once widely so employed. An old seed catalog described them as indispensable for all crops requiring potash, and of high value for cabbages, potatoes, onions, strawberries, fruit trees, corn, and beans. (Caution: ashes may encourage scab in potatoes.) A typical application was one pound of ashes for each 10 to 20 square feet. Hardwood ashes were always specified but those of soft woods are also of value if they have not been leached by rain. Old English farming advice from the late 18th century called for the collecting of all ashes—those from burning weeds, brush, rubbish, etc.—to be kept dry until spring seeding time, for use then, after the ashes were mixed with some soot and the whole thing was put through a sieve.

Samuel Deane included in 1790 among ashes for fertilizing, "coal ashes, top-dressing for cold, damp soils."

BONES

Because it lasts long in the soil and does not easily leach away in rainy spells even in sandy soil, bone has been a favored fertilizer for years. Bone meal is the form found today, but years ago bone was also supplied as ground bone and crushed bone. The old rule for the quantities to use was: one part bone to 50 of soil for a potting mix, or one pound of bone worked into 20 to 30 feet of row.

A gardener of the 1880s reported of her house plants that she gave them bone dust once a month. "I burn all the bones I get," she said, "then pound them fine." Burning the bones was not recommended by all. Seedsman Park advised his readers in May of 1886 to reduce bones with ashes in this way: "Put bones and ashes in alternate layers in an old barrel, moisten the whole with water and place it in a dry situation for several months. Fresh wood ashes must be used, and the compost kept continually moist." We would add that this mixture would not do to feed acid-loving plants. The same is true of an old English method reported by John Monk in 1794: "Mr. Paget recommends, instead of being at the expense and trouble of grinding the bones, to mix them in a heap with lime, which will in a short time reduce the bones to powder." Unslaked lime was used.

"Bones of all kinds pounded or broke into small pieces," were highly recommended by Deane. "This is an incomparable manure, if they have not been burnt, nor boiled in soap. . . . Sixty bushels are sufficient dressing for an acre." About a bucketful to 200 feet of row is a garden equivalent.

BURNED EARTH

Here is advice to American gardeners of 1821 by the English gardening authority William Cobbett: "Clay, or any earth, *burnt*, is excellent manure for a garden. It has no seeds of weeds or grass in it. A compost made of such ashes, some wood ashes, a small portion of horse dung, rotten leaves, and mould shoveled up under trees, round buildings, or on the sides of roads. All these together, put into a heap and turned over several times, make the best manure for a garden." The way earth was burned was to dig clods ahead of time, as in trimming up bed borders, and let them dry on the ground. Then a bonfire was made and when it was burning well, the dried clods were thrown on it. As the fire burned itself out, the burned clods mingled with the ashes, and the whole was then stored for future use. One bushel to 300 square feet was a common application.

CASTOR BEANS

If you grow the plant, you can use castor beans as a fertilizer. The crushed bean, a by-product from the extraction of the oil, was so used many years ago and is sometimes available today. Peter Henderson noted in 1881, "The pomace is used as a manure." The beans are poisonous if eaten, by the way, and have occasionally caused illness in children who were attracted to the beans by the bright coloring.

A Virginia gentleman farmer, T. G. Peachy of Williamsburg, was pioneering in castor bean meal as a fertilizer in the 1840s, and his experiments indicated that 40 bushels to the acre was an average requirement. A bucketful to 300 feet of garden row is a rough equivalent.

COFFEE GROUNDS

An experienced gardener of the post-Civil-War era observed: "Coffee grounds are excellent fertilizers. I have seen seedlings growing vigorously in the pure grounds and thriving equally with those planted in good earth." Our experience with coffee grounds is that they make a good mulch and are a welcome component of compost.

RIGHT: *Back in the days when even many city families kept a few chickens, the manure and the moulted feathers were sources of fertilizer for the garden.*

22

There is Money

in Poultry if you know how to get it,—it is good money.

100,000 people in America can make more money out of Poultry.

Our book, THE POULTRY YARD, HOW TO FURNISH AND MANAGE IT, tells what we know,—you know we study Poultry for profit.

The tenth edition is entirely remade.

Besides the descriptions of the leading Land and Water Fowls, it also contains chapters on the BEST PLANS OF POULTRY HOUSES,— HOW TO MAKE INCUBATORS,—SELECTION AND MATING OF STOCK,—WHAT AND HOW TO FEED,—GENERAL MANAGEMENT,— FRENCH METHOD OF KILLING,—DRESSING AND SHIPPING POULTRY,—EGGS AND CHICKENS, — DIRECTIONS FOR CAPONIZING, WITH PLAIN ILLUSTRATIONS,—DISEASES, WITH TRIED AND PROVEN PRESCRIPTIONS,—HOW TO RAISE GOOD TURKEYS, etc., etc.

Every book is good for some one.

If each one this book is good for could see it fifteen minutes they would buy it; then we doubt if the printer could supply us fast enough. You see it is the right book for so many people.

As it is, we can only ask all who want to make more money out of Poultry to take our word for it.

The cost of the book is as nothing compared with its value.

PRICE BY MAIL, POSTPAID, in handsomely designed paper covers, **50 cts.**, or bound in cloth, **75 cts.** or you can have a copy **FREE AS A PREMIUM** on any $5.00 or $7.50 order.

W. ATLEE BURPEE & CO., Philadelphia.

EGGSHELLS An old fertilizer for house plants was water in which crushed eggshells had been soaked for 24 hours. Eggshells contain calcium, which is a nutrient plants need, but we would add this caution: Do not give this solution to acid-loving plants, such as azaleas or gardenias, since excessive calcium (lime) is harmful to them.

FISH That famous Indian fertilizer, fish, was also on Deane's list. "Fish of all kinds, from the whale to the mussel; they are best used in composts, and should lie a year, that their oil may be dissolved and fitted for the nourishing of plants. . . . Shells of shell-fish, ploughed in whole, are a good manure for dry soils, and ground or pounded small, for stiff lands."

GREENSAND Greensand, found along the New Jersey and Virginia coasts, among other places, was being valued as a fertilizer by the first half of the 19th century. Greensand, a granular, half-soft marine deposit that contains about 6 percent of potash, is an olive-green iron-potassium silicate, also called glauconite. An old *Report of Geological Survey of New Jersey*, approximately from the 1840s, mentions the "luxurious harvests," resulting from use of "this curiously constituted mineral," and surmises that "There can be no doubt that the agriculture of our seaboard states is destined to derive essential benefit" from its use. Greensand is available today from a few natural-fertilizer companies.

HAIR "Hair," said Deane in 1790, was "a top-dressing for grassland; under the surface of a dry soil in tillage, or in compost. In either way it is an excellent fertilizer." Hair was recognized in Johnson's 1851 farming encyclopedia as of fertilizing value:

"The refuse hair of different animals, particularly the short hair from hides, and that of hogs, when it can be procured in sufficient quantity, will be found useful as fertilizer." He also quotes here a chemical analysis of hair, published some time after 1800 by a Mr. Vauquelin and saying that hair contained animal matter, two kinds of oil, iron, manganese, lime, silica, and sulfur.

Hair can be dug directly into the soil, but we have found it is more easily handled if included in the raw materials of compost.

HOOVES

Under the heading, "A Good Liquid Fertilizer," a periodical of the 1870s carried the following recommendation: "Put one bushel of the clippings from horses' hoofs into a barrel, and fill it up with water. Let it stand for a week, when it is fit for use. Apply it with a watering pot." The rate of application was about twice a week. "Two or three weeks after plants have been watered with the manure," the recommendation ran, "the foliage generally changes from green to a golden yellow, moving from the stem down to the point of the leaf, which, however, lasts only for a few weeks, when it changes to a dark glossy green. Plants under this watering grow strong; the flowers are very large and bright in color. Plants thus treated can be kept in very small pots for a long time without being transplanted. . . . The chips need be removed only twice a year—fall and spring." As the solution was dipped out, more water was added to the barrel. We question the fertilizing value of the solution, but offer the suggestion to the experimental reader who may have access to a farrier.

LEATHER

Being of animal origin, leather has been used for fertilizer, and Deane endorsed it, saying, "Leather, new or old, in small bits for dry soil," was worth having.

MANURES

Animals' manures were of course a standby as fertilizers years ago; there was so much of them. Even so, guano, the droppings of sea birds and some others, was imported by the shipload and was very highly regarded. Human wastes were being used to some extent in Europe one or two centuries ago, and what was found good in Europe was adopted in the New World if it worked here.

Composting of manures was good gardening practice; in farming operations, fresh manure might be spread on the land, to be ploughed in at once, a change from a practice in Tudor times in England, when Thomas Tusser wrote of the practice of exposing the spread manure to the weather for months before turning it under.

Summertime advice to southern California gardeners from Germain's in the 1890s was: "If manure is used, it should be in liquid form." The point here may have been to avoid raising soil temperature, although this would not be the case with composted manure. In any case, a manure solution or a compost solution gives plants a fast feeding and has been used for centuries.

MUD

"Pond mud or ditch scrapings" were a common and well-liked garden fertilizer during the 18th and 19th centuries—and for some centuries before, being recommended in the famed Thomas Tusser agricultural work, *A Hundreth Good Pointes of Husbandrie*, published in England in 1557. In 1851 Johnson was recommending these same fertilizers for potatoes, each cubic yard of them having added to it one bushel of bacon salt or common salt. The fertility of pond bottoms is well known, and an agricultural practice in some parts of the world is to drain ponds at intervals in order to grow crops on the bottoms.

RIGHT: *By the time the 19th century was nearing its end, interest in chemical fertilizers was high, and this booklet told gardeners how to mix their own—along with giving information on some of the tried-and-true natural fertilizers also described in this chapter.*

MANURES — How to Make and How to Use Them.

A Practical Treatise on the Chemistry of Manures and Manure Making.

This new book on the chemistry of manures and manure making is a really important work, written by FRANK W. SEMPERS, an expert agricultural chemist connected with FORDHOOK FARM, specially for the use of farmers, horticulturalists, and market gardeners. It clearly explains the principles underlying soil fertilization and the best methods for preparing natural and chemical manures on the farm and applying them. It has been demonstrated that chemical fertilization can be made on the farm, without the aid of machinery, with a great saving of expense. The different raw materials entering into the composition of the fertilizers are plainly described, and the best commercial sources of supply given. Considerable space is devoted to tried and proved formulas, drawing from the most practical results of the latest scientific researches in America, England, France, and Germany. In this connection is explained the meaning of chemical terms used in the State Agricultural Reports and the general agricultural and horticultural literature of the day. The arrangement and classification are in accordance with the best scientific usage, and every formula is the result of actual field experiment. No formulas based on theoretical estimates have been admitted into the book. The preparation of this book has involved a large amount of careful work, and we have no hesitation in saying it is the best book on the subject. **PRICE, POSTPAID, 50 CTS.**

FREE AS A PREMIUM. Any $5.00 order can, if desired by the purchaser, include, entirely free, a copy of this new book; or, if your order amounts to $2.00, you can get it for 30 cts. added. ☞ As stated on **PAGE 9**, we allow a **credit of 10 cts. on each Dollar** to apply to the purchase of **any of our Books**—or if preferred, this same credit may apply toward a subscription to GARDENING—the new horticultural magazine—advertised below.☜

"AS OTHERS SEE US." ☞ We would invite special attention to our offer of **thirty-four Cash Prizes, amounting to SIX HUNDRED AND FIFTY-FIVE DOLLARS,** which we will pay to the writers of the best articles on our business, seeds, etc. For full particulars **see page 132.**

THE WORLD'S FAIR. We would also ask attention to the announcement on **page 12,** that we have arranged to offer **OVER ONE THOUSAND DOLLARS** in Cash Prizes for the best products of **BURPEE'S SEEDS** that our customers may exhibit at The World's Columbian Exposition, in Chicago.

GARDENING

GARDENING is devoted to plain gardening matters in plain language that the least informed can readily understand. It aims to tell Amateurs in gardening what they want to know, in the way they want to be told. It is edited by WILLIAM FALCONER, who is universally recognized to be the best informed practical gardener in America. He has charge of the beautiful Dosoris Gardens (50 acres in extent) at Glen Cove, Long Island, where the very best possible results are attained in every department of practical and ornamental gardening. Mr. Falconer has studied gardening from the Amateur's standpoint all his life, and he will freely give to the readers of GARDENING the practical results of his long experience, without any reservation. He is ably assisted by contributors who have thorough practical knowledge of the subjects assigned to them. The paper is very freely illustrated, with the object of making quite plain any points that might otherwise be difficult to understand. It is the journal that all lovers of gardening have needed and waited for. It is issued twice a month. Sample copy mailed on receipt of stamp. Subscription price $1.00 a year (24 numbers); or six months for 50 cents.

W. ATLEE BURPEE & CO., PHILADELPHIA, PA.

OILS

Deane recommended "Oil of all sorts, used in compost, not applied to the soil till a year after it is mixed." For oil here, read animal fats and vegetable oils. Whale oil and blubber were once accepted fertilizers.

RAGS

Cloth rags also received Deane's approval. "Linen rags," he said, "will be a manure worth having, but they take a long time to putrefy. Woolen rags, chopped to pieces," he said, were good for a light soil. "They should be as small as an inch square. Twenty-four bushels are said to be a sufficient quantity for the dressing of an acre." This is roughly equivalent to one bushel for a 20′ by 75′ garden (1500 square feet). Another source said that 1350 pounds per acre was a good rate. Farmers said the woolen rags "warmed the land" and lasted about two years. Both old and new rags were used but older ones were preferred, and if they had absorbed much perspiration, so much the better. The method of cutting them was by use of a chopper and block.

SALT

Common salt was being used as a fertilizer years ago, and with apparently good results, although to today's gardeners this may come as a shock. After all, salt is usually a good way to *kill* a plant, such as a weed. But in an 1864 farmer's almanac, readers were instructed to mix seven bushels of salt with seven bushels of soot, to be ploughed into one acre of ground. This is at a rate of one quart of the mixture to every 100 square feet of soil.

Johnson in 1851 made the observation that "the brine of pickling tubs, when poured over heaps of weeds, not only killed those weeds and their attendant seeds and grubs, but these heaps were then converted into so many parcels of the most fertilizing manure, whose good effects, especially upon potatoes and carrots, were very decided." From his use of the word "heaps," he appears to be describing a composting process.

And in the 1840s Henry Ward Beecher put the case for salt this way: "Salt may be used with great advantage on all garden soils, but especially upon light and sandy ones. Thus treated, soils will resist summer drouths and be moist when otherwise they would suffer. Salt has also a good effect in destroying vermin, and it adds valuable chemical ingredients to the soil."

SALTPETER

Known from ancient times, saltpeter, which is potassium nitrate, has been valued as a fertilizer for centuries. It forms a part of some commercial fertilizers today, in fact. Saltpeter occurs in the earth of certain regions.

SAWDUST

Sawdust as a garden fertilizer came to notice in the first half of the 19th century. It was generally composted along with manures or vegetation, but another way to use it, described by Johnson, was: "When mixed with blood and quicklime it forms an excellent manure." Sawdust is a good source of carbon in a compost pile, especially of use when mixed with fresh grass clippings.

SEAWEED

For those who can gather it, seaweed is a valuable fertilizer and mulch. Here is what Deane had to say of it in 1790:

> Ore-weed, sea-weed, sea-ware, or sea-wreck; These names are applied to all the vegetables which grow plentifully in the sea and on the muddy and rocky parts of the shore below high water mark.
>
> All vegetables when putrefied are a good pabulum for plants; for they consist wholly of it. But the value of marine vegetables is greater than that of any other: for, besides the virtues of the other, they contain a large quantity of salt, which is a great fertilizer. Mr. Dixon thinks those weeds which grow in the deepest water are the best. Perhaps they

contain a greater proportion of salt than those which grow near the shore, as they are seldom or never wetted with fresh water.

I rather think it is best to putrefy sea-weeds before they are applied to the soil. This may speedily be accomplished by laying it in heaps. But the heaps should not lie naked. Let them be covered with loose earth or turf; or else mixed in compost dung-hills with divers other substances. It will soon dissolve itself and what is mixed with it, changing to a salt oily slime, very proper to fertilize light soils, and not improper for almost any other.

One disadvantage attending the business of farming in this country is, that our cold winters put an entire stop to the fermentation, and putrefaction of manures. This may be in some measure obviated by the use of rock-weed, which is so full of salt that it is not easily frozen. I have been informed that some have laid it under their dung hills by the sides of barns; in which situation it has not frozen; but by its fermentation has dissolved itself, and much of the dung that lay upon it. There is undoubtedly a great advantage in such a practice.

Another advantage of this kind of manure is that it does not encourage the growth of weeds so much as dung. It is certain it has none of the seeds of weeds to propagate, as dung almost always has.

This manure is represented in the Complete Farmer to be twice as valuable as dung, if cut from the rocks at low water mark; that a dressing of it will last three years;—and that fruit trees which have been barren are rendered fruitful by laying this manure about their roots.

SOLUBLE FERTILIZERS

Soluble fertilizers are not as new as they may seem. Nearly 100 years ago, in 1877, this formula appeared in the *Floral Cabinet*, a publication addressed to flower growers: "The following works like magic on vegetable life. You can recommend it without fear of injury. Ammonium sulphate 4 oz.; saltpetre 2 oz.; white sugar 1 oz.; powder, mix, and dissolve in 1 qt. of water. Add one tablespoon of this mixture to one gallon of water, and water the plants with it once or twice a week." The significant fertilizers this mixture contained were nitrogen, potash, and sulfur; it lacked phosphorus and was quite dilute.

A common form of soluble fertilizer was manure water. Composted or old manure was generally used, a gunny sack half full of it being hung in a barrel of water. When the water was the color of tea it was used to feed plants. Compost may also be so used.

SOOT

An 1878 suggestion was: "A good liquid fertilizer is formed by mixing a quart or two of wood-soot from the stove pipe or chimney to a barrel of water and letting it stand for twenty-four hours previous to using." Soot was also sprinkled on the earth as a fertilizer, "increasing luxuriousness of growth," an old seed catalog stated, "and giving darkness and brilliance to foliage and flowers."

So-called soot tea became a soluble fertilizer for house plants: "I give my plants soot tea once a week," a 19th-century gardener stated, and this formula for soot tea was given by a rose grower of the same period: "I place about a peck of soot in a half-barrel in some convenient place near the garden, fill this with water and use it once a week around the roots of the roses, thoroughly wetting the ground with it. Keep filling the barrel up with water as you take it out, and it will remain strong enough to use the whole summer."

THREE

Old-Fashioned Pest Controls
for a Modern Environment

PESTS in the forms of insects, animal life, and plant diseases are older than gardening. In this chapter we take up some of the formidable number of weapons our ancestors used against the pests, often with more success than today's pesticides offer, and nearly always without contaminating side effects and threats to man's own health and safety.

The order of arrangement is an alphabetical listing of pests, using modern names wherever an old one would be unfamiliar.

ANTS

"Fresh guano sprinkled upon the ground in which ants are troublesome," it was reported by a gardener in 1879, "is said to be effectual in driving them away. When they affect plants, give them a shower-bath of water in which potash has been dissolved, using an ounce of potash to a pail of water." Wood ashes contain about five percent of potash (but should not be used on acid-loving plants).

Peter Henderson's remedy was: "Saturate pieces of sponge

32

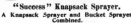

PETER HENDERSON & CO. NEW YORK · FOUNDED 1847.

IMPLEMENTS APPLYING INSECTICIDES & FUNGICIDES

"SUCCESS" KNAPSACK SPRAYER.

"FRUITALL" SPRAYING PUMP.

"Fruitall" Spraying Outfit.

A simple, high grade, up-to-date pump, embodying several important improvements. All working parts of brass. It can be mounted on or removed from barrel by two thumbscrews. Air chamber of unusually large capacity. A long, adjustable handle. It is low down and within the barrel, offering no obstruction to limbs, and is not top-heavy. The pump is large, but easily operated by a single person. The agitator is mechanical in action, much superior to the old "return discharge." The most efficient and satisfactory spray pump ever offered. (See cut.) "Fruitall" Outfit "A." Pump with one lead 10 feet ½-inch discharge hose with "Vermorel" Spray Nozzle and Agitator, $9.50. Price does not include barrel.

Iron Extension Pipe, 8 feet, with stopcock, (for tree spraying) fitted to attach to nozzle and hose, $1.50 extra.

"Henderson" Hand Bucket Pump.

This is the best and most durable portable hand pump. Working parts of solid brass; large air chamber; is double-acting, throwing a continuous stream, either solid or in a fine spray, as desired; very light and easily carried, and works from any bucket or tub. Just the thing for throwing liquid insecticides and fungicides on low trees, shrubs, plants, etc., and by altering the nozzle it can be used for washing carriages, windows, etc. (See cut.) Price, $3.75; or, with extra 7 feet section of hose and pole connection for tree spraying, $4.75.

HENDERSON'S BUCKET PUMP.

"Acme" Spraying Outfit.

A very complete and convenient outfit for spraying garden crops, flowers, shrubs, vineyards, etc. The hardwood iron-hooped tank holds about 25 gallons, is firmly fastened to a cart narrow enough for most garden paths; it is easily wheeled about and sits firmly while the pump is being operated. The force-pump has brass cylinder, to prevent corrosion when fungicides are used. Price, complete, cart, pump, 4 feet discharge hose and combination spray and stream nozzle, $10.00. Iron extension pipe, 8 feet (for tree spraying), fitted to attach to nozzle and hose, $1.50 extra.

"ACME" SPRAYING OUTFIT.

Champion Dry Powder Gun.

For applying any dry powder, such as Paris green, hellebore, insect powder, plaster, etc., on plants or trees, the powder being evenly distributed over a wide space and with the least possible waste, the work being more rapidly done than by any other known implement. It is 27 inches long, with extra tubes for dusting trees, and holds one quart of powder. By turning the crank it is rapidly revolved, which forces a current of air through the tubes, that carries with it a small portion of powder. The quantity may be increased or diminished, as desired. (See cut.) Price, complete, $7.50.

Little Giant Powder Gun.

Improved for 1900—similar to the "Champion," but smaller, and dusts only one row. Price, $5.00.

"Success" Knapsack Sprayer.

A Knapsack Sprayer and Bucket Sprayer Combined.

For applying fungicides and insecticides in a mist-like spray, for the treatment of mildew, black rot on grapes, as well as for potato blight, etc. With it a man can spray five to six acres of vines in a day. The machines are made entirely of copper and brass, and the chemicals will not corrode or rust them. The air chamber keeps up a steady pressure, so a continuous discharge is given. The new improvements enable this sprayer to be used either as a knapsack or bucket sprayer. The Pump may be worked with either the right or left hand. Any leakage around the plunger is returned into the tank, and does not run down the operator's back. The attachment shown at A is for underspraying. Price, complete, as shown in cut, $11.00.

Paris Green Sprinkler.

A five-gallon galvanized iron sprayer for applying poisonous fluids to vines, bushes, potatoes, etc. Can be carried either on the back or by hand. The fluid flows through the rubber tube and is forced out like rain by pressing the rubber bulb held in the hand; this spray will reach 10 to 12 feet. Price, $2.50; or, with double sprinkling attachment for two rows at once, $3.50.

PARIS GREEN SPRINKLER.

Woodason's Double Cone Powder Bellows.

For dusting plants with dry powders. Can be held in any direction without wasting powder, and does not clog up. The best bellows for destroying insects in conservatory, garden, orchard or field; it dusts under the leaves as well as on top. (See cut.) Price, $2.75.

Single Cone Powder Bellows.

Price, large size, $1.75. Small size (for conservatory and house use), $1.00.

Woodason's Fluid Vaporizing Bellows.

For spraying plants with fluid decoctions for insects and fungus. Throws a spray as fine as mist. (See cut.) Price, large size, $2.00. Small size (for house use), $1.25.

The Asbestos Torch.

Attach the torch to the end of a pole of suitable length; saturate with kerosene oil, light and hold under the caterpillars' nests and pass quickly along the branches and around the trunk of the tree where the insects lodge. The heat instantly destroys the insects and will in no way injure the tree. Price, 40c. each; or by mail, 50c.

ASBESTOS TORCH.

Norton's Plant Duster.

For dusting potatoes, vines, etc. An air-chamber prevents clogging. The dust guard prevents the powder from escaping beyond the plant being treated. Price, 85c. each.

Henderson's Atomizing Syringe.

For spraying fluids or powders. The reservoir of heavy copper is not corroded by chemicals. Just what is needed for applying insecticides and fungicides in a mist-like vapor. Holds one pint; length of barrel, 19 ins.; diameter, 1¾ ins. Each, $1.00.

NORTON'S PLANT DUSTER.

WOODASON'S BELLOWS, FOR POWDER AND FLUID.

ATOMIZING SYRINGE COPPER RESERVOIR APPLIES BOTH FLUIDS & POWDER.

LEGGETT'S CHAMPION DRY POWDER GUN.

OUR IMPLEMENT CATALOGUE (mailed free on application) ILLUSTRATES AND DESCRIBES A FULL LINE OF HORSE AND HAND POWER SPRAYING IMPLEMENTS.

By 1900 the gardener was being offered a variety of patented sprays and dusters intended to make pest control more effective. Those shown on this page from the old Peter Henderson & Company seed catalog show various sprayers, dusters, and a torch that was used to burn web caterpillars infesting trees.

with sugar, or place fresh bones around their haunts; they will leave everything else to feed on these, and when they are thus trapped, can be destroyed by dipping in hot water or burning." A like method that was being used in the 1840s was to heat the fleshy side of a bacon rind and place it on the ground under a stone. It was plunged into a pail of water when covered with ants. An 1870s ant trap was a flowerpot inverted over the ant hill. After a day or two, when the pot was well populated with ants on their way in or out of the nest, the pot was plunged into boiling water. Another ant fighter was sulfur sprinkled on affected plants. (Don't put sulfur on the garden vine plants such as squash, as it may kill them.) Still another weapon against ants was a chalk line drawn around a plant; this was used for fruit trees espaliered against a house wall, and another broad band of chalkline was made on the wall near ground level.

APHIDS

In the summer of 1787 Samuel Deane reported in his farmer's dictionary that he found the best way of getting rid of aphids was to place elder branches (presumably those of the elderberry) in the affected plants. He did not say whether the elders were a repellent or a counter-attraction, but were presumably a repellent.

Tobacco dust was being used in the mid-19th century against aphids on chrysanthemums and other plants. For house plants bothered by aphids, some gardeners blew tobacco smoke through the foliage.

A treatment used in the last century against aphids was a spray of one tablespoon of kerosene in a quart of lukewarm water, washed off with plain water the day after.

A late-19th century gardener in West Virginia observed: "It is said that the water in which tomato leaves and stems have been boiled, will, if sprinkled over plants which are infected with aphis and other pests, effectually destroy the pests. The leaves of the China Tree and also a decoction of oak bark are said to be equally efficacious for this purpose."

34

"Green fly" was another word for aphids, according to Peter Henderson in 1881, and root aphids were called blue aphids. The latter were attacked with a solution of tobacco stems boiled in water to the color of coffee, cooled, and poured at the base of the plant.

Early in the present century a kerosene emulsion was used against aphids and other sucking insects. There were two ways of making it. One was to beat two parts of kerosene with one part of sour milk until the mixture thickened. It was then diluted with 20 parts of water and used at once. For a longer-keeping mixture, a half-pound of laundry soap was cut up in a gallon of water, then boiled until the soap dissolved. This was taken off the stove, two gallons of kerosene were added, and the mixture was churned for five minutes or until thick and creamy. It would keep indefinitely. One cup of it mixed with 20 cups (five quarts) of water made the right strength of spray.

BARK INSECTS

A gardening magazine's advice in 1898 to a correspondent complaining of a white "scaly bug" on apple tree trunks was: "One of the best remedies for bark insects is a solution of sal-soda. Make a rather strong solution and apply it by means of a bristle white-wash brush. It may be effectually applied either to ornamental shrubs and trees or to fruit trees."

BARK PESTS

In the middle of the 19th century the trunks of fruit trees that were being bothered by blights or by bark insects were given a coat of clay-and-water. The mixture was made the consistency of cream and put on with a brush.

BIRDS

In the interest of those who are pained to hear of birds being treated as enemies, we would like to quote a bit from the 1851 farmer's encyclopedia of Cuthbert Johnson: "In one of the English counties where the rook (a bird allied to the crow) had increased so as to do some damage to the crops, a destructive war was waged against them, so that they were nearly exterminated. But under these circumstances various species of the insect tribe increased so rapidly that it became necessary to import the rooks again from the adjoining counties."

An old device to keep birds from eating cherries was to spray the developing fruit with a weak salt-water solution.

This simple plot to keep birds out of the garden was being used in the 18th century and probably was old then. A bell was fastened to a post set in the garden, and a cord ran from the bell to the house kitchen. Whoever happened to pass the cord gave it a yank, ringing the bell and scaring off any bird that happened to be in the garden.

CATERPILLARS

White, or false, hellebore, an insecticide that is not really hellebore but is derived from the Veratrum plant, was a popular control years ago for slugs, caterpillars, and other leaf-eating pests. It was used as a dust, or was dissolved, one ounce to three gallons of water, for a spray. It is safe enough to apply even when vegetables or fruits are nearly ripe. (True hellebore, a constituent of the Christmas rose, is toxic to people.)

Small caterpillars on roses were attacked by sprinkling the plants with soot, sometimes mixed with white hellebore.

Mercury was once considered by some an insect repellent, and to keep webworms from apple trees, a hole was bored a third way through the trunk, a drop or two of mercury put in, and a peg stopper inserted. Some said this kept the tree free from attack. Others who tried it were not convinced. Our own opinion is that no good would come of it—and mercury is none too safe to handle anyway.

Deane reported in 1790 that he had kept webworms out of his orchard by hanging wet rock weed in the trees. This was seaweed that clung to shoreline rocks. He hung it in the crotches of the trees in April, and reasoned that the salty water dripping from it helped the trees resist the insect attack. It seems more likely that the seaweed may have repelled the moths that laid the caterpillar eggs. At any rate, by the time he reported on the experiment he had tried it twice and was satisfied it was effective.

Although not universally popular with gardeners, wasps are valuable friends when they destroy caterpillars. Social wasps build a papery nest, shown above.

A forerunner to Tanglefoot as a sticky band around trees was made from rubber. Johnson described it in 1851: "Let a piece of Indian rubber be burnt over a gallipot [pottery jar] into which it will gradually drop in the condition of a viscid juice, which state, it appears, it will always retain. . . . Let a piece of cord or worsted be smeared with it, and then tied several times around the trunk. The melted substance is so very sticky that the insects will be prevented, and generally captured, in their attempts to pass over it."

CUCUMBER
BEETLES

A Dr. B. S. Barton of Philadelphia was quoted in the mid-19th century as recommending sprinkling cucumber vines with a mixture of tobacco and red pepper to rid them of cucumber beetles, and this was said to have worked well. Other weapons of the day for the beetles were teas made of tobacco, elder leaves, walnut leaves, or hops. One curious tactic was to stick lighted splinters of pine knots in the earth around the plants at night to attract and incinerate the beetles. (See also Striped Cucumber Beetle.)

CLUBROOT

Clubroot is a fungus disease that attacks the roots of plants of the cabbage group. Although the cause was not understood when Peter Henderson wrote his *Handbook of Plants* in 1881, he knew the problem very well, and reported he had successfully combated it by treating the soil, either mixing oyster shells with it in the previous fall or working bone dust in just before spring planting.

Ten years earlier an English gardening oracle, Mrs. Isabella Beeton, reasoned that cabbage suffered clubroot because it was a heavy feeder, so prevention called for extra manuring and rotation with soil-restoring crops. She also suggested dipping roots, before transplanting, in a mixture of two quarts of soot and a pound of saltpeter in enough water to make a thick paste.

CUTWORMS

"Salt is the best thing to kill cutworms outdoors," a Massachusetts gardener declared in 1886. "If you have a flower that they like pretty well put salt around the plant, stir it well into the soil, and your plant is saved. This has been tried by me for three years and has never failed." Salt, as we have said, is not good for most plants, and we would go cautiously here. Another anti-cutworm treatment was to crush eggshells and work them into the soil around plants.

Soot sprinkled on the garden was also said to drive cutworms off. So was a mixture of equal parts of salt, ashes, and plaster of Paris, or just salt and ashes.

In the 1840s a Pennsylvania man said he protected cabbage transplants from cutworms by wrapping stems with a hickory or walnut leaf.

The ever-resourceful Henry Ward Beecher used weeds as guard plants against cutworms that were after his tomatoes and cabbages. "If the weeds are kept down just about the hill," he said, "and permitted to grow for a few weeks between the rows, although it has a very slovenly look it will save the cabbages etc., by giving ample foot [food?] to the cutworm. When the plant grows tough in the stem the weeds may be lightly spaded in and the surface leveled with the rake."

EARTHWORMS

Although now generally regarded as friends, earthworms were not so regarded by many gardeners of the last century, especially when the worms inhabited the earth of potted plants. One remedy suggested was at least simpler than many: "Water the plant with the water in which potatoes have been boiled."

For outdoor plants, lime water was a popular earthworm killer.

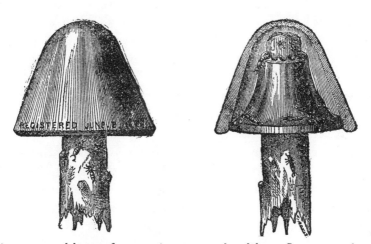

A century-old trap for earwigs, somewhat like a flowerpot placed upside down on a low post.

EARWIGS

The earwig was common enough in England during America's early days, and it gradually entered this country, although it was

39

not yet a pest in the mid-19th century. Nor is it yet in every part of the United States. The English gardeners trapped earwigs, and this is still a good method. Traps used were the hooves of animals and hollow reeds. These, laid about the garden or hung in fruit trees, lured earwigs at the approach of dawn, and were gathered during the day and dropped into hot water or brine. A rolled-up newspaper will do the same service today, and can be burned. Another trap once used was a small flowerpot with a little dry moss stuffed into the bottom; this was hung upside down on a short stick among the plants to be protected, then emptied into boiling water in the morning when the earwigs were hidden in it.

FLEA BEETLES

Flea beetles, which attack brassicas, tomatoes, and many other plants, eating many small holes in the leaves, were treated a century ago by spraying affected plants with a soap solution or with a solution of wormwood. Sometimes it was put on with a sprinkling can. A soap application should be followed with one of plain water within an hour. To make a solution of wormword or of any plant so used, pour a quart of boiling water over a quart of the leaves, let steep for an hour, drain off the liquid and mix with a gallon of water; use at once.

A curious alternative to the spraying for flea beetles was the use of a net. Johnson described it: "Great numbers of the beetles may be caught by the skillful use of a deep bag-net of muslin, which should be swept over the plants." The captured beetles were then crushed. The gardener was warned not to use the net over tender young plants lest they be bruised or broken.

FLIES

An English gardeners' magazine of about 1850 gave this fly-killer advice: "A mixture of pepper, sugar, and water will speedily attract and destroy flies and waspes." Wasps are gardeners' friends, as they destroy caterpillars, but they weren't very popular with yesterday's gardeners, probably especially those who had been stung.

GRUBS

Writing in 1787, New England's Samuel Deane recommended that the best way known to get rid of grubs in the soil was to spade or plough so that the birds could get at the exposed pests. This is still good advice. A year-around mulch is not good garden practice in every location, as this suggests, if it harbors pests that cannot be got at under the protection of the mulch.

In the late 19th century, soot spread on the soil was thought to repel grubs.

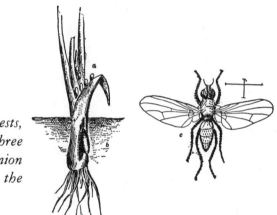

Maggots, the constant pests, shown here in the three phases: eggs, laid on an onion leaf; larva working on the root; the adult, a fly.

MAGGOTS

The maggot fly is not only a current plague—it was so common a pest 200 years ago, it even figured in a practical joke an English con man pulled on gullible countrymen, selling for a guinea a "secret way" to destroy the fly. It was: "Roll them in the night with a heavy roller."

"My radishes sown early seldom escape; those sown in June mostly prosper," said an American gardener of the 1780s. He also mentioned a method a friend had tried, treating cabbage plants that were already invaded by maggots. He watered them with sea water and found this stopped the attack. Deane suggested that inland gardeners try a brine solution. Again, we advise caution with use of salt.

41

An 1886 gardener said, "I have found nothing that exterminates them so well as lime water." A fist-sized lump of lime in a bucket of water was the formula. Another gardener of this era said she killed maggots by pouring boiling water on the earth of pot plants; "That is, in small quantity," she added, "so as not to injure the roots."

A seed treatment from the 1780s was intended to guard seedlings against maggot-fly attack: "To a quart of turnip seed add one ounce of brimstone finely powdered, putting both in a bottle large enough to afford room to shake them well together every day for four or five days previous to sowing; keep the bottle well corked. This has, by long experience, been proved never to fail." Brimstone was the old word for sulfur.

Another seed treatment was to soak seeds in whale oil for 24 hours before sowing; any vegetable oil would also serve, it was said, and the treatment was thought to speed growth of plants.

A third seed treatment against maggots, from this same period, was to bruise fresh elder leaves in a mortar until sufficient oil was extracted to cover the seeds; they were soaked in it overnight and planted the next day along with the leaves.

Branches of elder were also used against maggots, being raked across the seed bed after sowing. It was supposed the maggot fly disliked the odor, and if this is so, a mulch of elder branches would be helpful. One gardener of the late-18th century said to bruise the branches first, or treat them with "the smoak of burnt tobacco mixed with a small quantity of assafoetida."

Soot was also sprinkled around plants to repel the maggot fly.

To keep the fly from his turnips, one 18th-century gardener sowed seed on land covered by trash mulch—plants left strewn on the earth after stirring it with rake or harrow. His reasoning was that the weeds concealed the turnip seedlings from the maggot fly and were easily hoed off later.

Another tactic against maggots was the use of fresh seed, as it was felt it grew stronger plants and "healthy and vigorous

42

plants escape the fly," a gardener noted in 1788.

This interesting variation in timing was also used: When sowing turnips, old seed was mixed with new seed; the new came up three or four days ahead of the old and was attacked by the maggot fly; when the old seed sprouted, those seedlings escaped attack, presumably because the maggot fly thought she had already taken care of the entire planting. An alternate method was to divide the turnip seed into two parts, using all new or all old seed, and soak one part in water for five or six hours; the soaked and unsoaked seed were sown in the same row; the soaked seed sprouted first and was attacked by the fly, sparing most of the later-sprouting plants.

Mustard was another weapon against maggots; one teaspoon of it was mixed with a pint of water and poured around an affected plant. This was reported in the 1880s and was being used with house plants; another treatment substituted a few drops of carbolic acid for the mustard.

In the late 19th century, seedman W. Atlee Burpee suggested the still-used protector: "A piece of tarred paper placed around the stem of the young plant is fairly effective in preventing the maggots from reaching the roots." A 3″ square of the paper with a hole for the plant in the center was placed flat on the soil at the base of the plant.

MEALY BUGS

Mealy bugs on roses were sprayed with the hellebore solution described for caterpillars.

MILDEW

In the 1880s mildew on flowers was treated with a spray of sulfide of potassium, one ounce to a gallon of water, late in the evening, and in the morning plants were sprayed with plain water and given plenty of air.

In 1886 a New York State woman gave this treatment for tea roses: "I use sulfur sifted on dry after watering, for mildew."

MITES

To destroy the Eucharis mite, the editor of *Park's Floral Magazine* recommended the sulfide of potassium spray given above for mildew. The mite was destructive to bulbs of the Eucharis, lily, amaryllis, and other fleshy-rooted plants, he said, and the treatment "will also be found valuable in ridding the soil of other pests."

Kerosene emulsion (see Aphids) was also used against mites.

MISCELLANEOUS PESTS

"I keep a bottle of tobacco water handy to banish plant vermin," said a gardener of the 1880s. "I also use carbolic acid, 15 drops in a pint of water, and sprinkle the affected plants." But another gardener of the time said she had killed 40 cineraria plants with the same treatment; "I suppose I put it on too strong," she concluded.

"Alum water sprinkled on plants two or three times a week," claimed an 1877 gardener, "will kill any kind of insect there may be in the earth, and it is much less troublesome than baking the earth."

An 1886 California gardener said "I have got rid of several insect pests by simply placing tomato leaves among the plants infested. The black fleas or bugs did not stay on the plants ten minutes after placing leaves among them."

A dusting of soot early in the morning on young melon plants was practiced in the 19th century as a protection against destructive insects. This same measure would apply to related plants such as cucumbers and squash.

"An infusion of wormwood or a decoction of almost any other bitter plant sprinkled on vegetables, it is asserted, will prevent [insects] from eating them," said Deane in 1790.

Soap was used against insects on fruit trees. Whale-oil soap was favored, and in the 1900 Peter Henderson catalog it was offered at 15 cents a pound. Most gardeners of that and earlier times depended on homemade lye soap for the purpose, however. Three ways of employing the soap were these: First, it was used in a wash, scrubbing the trunk and limbs with a stiff brush or a wad of burlap, to eradicate eggs or hibernating insects under loose bark. The second use was as a band around the trunk to discourage crawling insects from climbing the tree; the soap was simply smeared on the trunk. The third method was to tie bars of soap around the trunk, about halfway between ground level and lowest limbs; this served as a repellent for crawling insects, and the rain washing some soap onto the trunk and earth was thought to prevent some insect attacks.

This helpful footnote appeared in the September, 1879, issue of *Park's Floral Magazine*: "Toads are useful in either greenhouse or garden to destroy insects. They are innocent and amusing little creatures, and the good they do the florist is incalculable."

An old general pesticide, long in use, is tobacco. You can buy it as dust, or in liquid concentrate as nicotine sulfate. The nicotine in both is a stomach poison and a contact poison for insects. You can also raise you own tobacco for the purpose. Start plants indoors in early spring as you do other tender crops. Prepare the garden bed by spading in a thin sprinkling of wood ashes two weeks ahead of transplanting; at transplanting time spade in 6" of compost and give each plant ¼ cup of cottonseed meal, spacing plants 3' apart. "When the flower stalks appear," old advice ran, "break them off and later remove the sprouts which start out at the base of the leaves, so that the full strength is thrown into the large leaves."

Curing the leaves can begin when yellow patches start appearing on them. Snip off each such leaf and hang it stem up in a carport, airy shed, or any place where it will stay *dry* and ventilated. Shred the leaves when fully dried, and store in closed containers such as coffee cans. To make a spray, soak one cup of shredded leaves in one gallon of water for an hour or so, strain off, mix liquid with one cup of soap flakes, and use at once. Put the spent leaves in your compost or use as a mulch. They are a mild fertilizer.

Powdered tobacco was recommended for pot plant insects by a gardener writing in 1886 to Park's magazine: "To prevent the coming of insects, put about once a month a pinch of powdered tobacco on the earth in the pots. The fumes of the tobacco, when watering, appears to be sufficient to keep the annoying pests away."

Tobacco seed is carried by Field, Olds, Shumway, and Stokes.

This tactic against insects on rose bushes was being used in the mid-19th century: "Take a shovel of live coals of fire, split open a red pepper and lay on the coals, and hold so that the smoke will go through the bush."

Red peppers were also used to make a repellent spray for various insects. Today a simple way is to mix a cup of peppers and two cups of water in a blender, let the mixture stand for a day, strain off the liquid and store it in the refrigerator. To use, add a gallon of water to ½ cup of the solution. Don't use this spray on tender young plants.

We recently heard of a gardener who merely planted hot peppers here and there among flowers and vegetables in his garden to ward off destructive worms. He said the pests left the vicinity after one taste of a pepper plant, no matter what part of it they attacked. (This device of repelling, rather than destroying, pests was in common use years ago, as many of the foregoing methods testify to.)

One pest control much in vogue among today's chemical-eschewing gardeners was not consciously practiced years ago. This is companion planting—the mingling of different sorts of plants in a single bed with the thought this will discourage some pests. As it happened, however, companion planting was done, especially in early days, when an intensive use of dooryard garden space was the rule.

Soapsuds were frequently used during the 19th century to water plants and kill pests. The subject received an extended airing in Park's magazine during 1886. One correspondent complained that a plant so treated had died, and another questioned if the suds had not been adulterated, saying that a friend's hired girl had washed a ham sack in water that she then used on plants, the plants thereupon losing leaves; she attributed this to the salt from the sack. In the April issue a California woman wrote: "Has anyone lost plants by watering with suds made from patent soap? . . . No more soapsuds for me, unless I use home-made soap." In the September issue a New York State woman concluded the discussion sensibly, saying of soapsuds: "I have never had any ill effects from using it on soil, but don't generally put it on foliage unless to kill insects, and then wash it off with clear water afterwards."

Yesterday's gardeners accepted a certain amount of plant damage from pests as inevitable. To make sure of having a good stand of plants, they seeded thickly. "I want to be sure of having plants enough for the worms and the bugs," one said. "As the plants grow, thin out the weak ones and all that have been attacked by the bugs." It was also realized that the pests were less trouble some times than other times, and referring to turnips and rutabagas, old advice noted that "when the plants get into the rough leaf, the danger from the black beetle is about over."

MOLES

"The castor oil bean is the best thing we ever tried," a gardener reported as to mole control in the late 19th century. "Last spring I went over our grounds and with a trowel opened the mole tracks, put in a few beans and covered them. This operation I repeated several times in the course of a few weeks. . . . We

47

were scarcely troubled with the little torments the rest of the summer." The gardener added that a cat was worth its weight in gold for catching moles. The cat must be interested and persistent, however.

Another gardener advised making the holes two or three feet apart with a pointed stick, and dropping four castor beans in each.

Perhaps it is in order here to put in a word in the mole's defense. He is an insect eater (the gopher, on the other hand, is a vegetarian), and when the insects the mole eats are destructive ones, he does the gardener a favor. A gardening magazine of the 1880s reported: "It is said that in a certain locality in France the chafer grubs became so numerous and destructive that gardening had to be given up. To rid the gardens of the pest a number of moles were introduced and in the course of a season or two the culturists were enabled to raise good crops."

A gardener of 1886 reported this mole-foiling method in Kentucky, used with tulips: "Plant the bulbs in old tin pans, then sink them in the beds." Pans, bulbs, and all were taken up and stored after the tulips had bloomed and the foliage had matured.

Here is a mole repellent used by a Maryland gardener in the 1880s: "I place the heads of salted herring in the ridges where the moles run. I find this an effectual remedy."

A mole chaser being used in the 1860s and earlier was to place elder leaves in the runs. The moles were said to abandon such runs, the odor of the elder being offensive to them.

POTATO BUGS

Explaining to a questioner the use of Paris green to kill potato bugs, the editor of Park's magazine said in 1879: "Mix with water, keep well stirred and apply with a fine sprinkler. Paris green is a rank poison, and must be handled with care." No proportions were given, but one teaspoon of Paris green to three gallons of water makes a mild insecticide. It was also employed against slugs, caterpillars, and other pests.

When used as a dust, the method was to mix 100 parts of flour to one part of Paris green; two cups of flour mixed with one teaspoon of Paris green would give you this proportion. Don't do the measuring with any spoon you use in the kitchen, of course.

RED SPIDER

Plain water was used years ago as a weapon against the red spider, a mite. "The spider does not like water, or a moist location," advised a gardening publication of the past century, "and many persons rid their plants by sprinkling occasionally with water."

To kill red spider on flowers, a gardener of the 1870s advised spraying with a tablespoon of kerosene mixed with one quart of lukewarm water, followed by a spraying of plain water the next day. A decade later another gardener reported that she sprinkled the ground around her rose bushes with tobacco tea whenever she saw a sign of red spiders, and said it always drove them away.

SCALE

Always a difficult pest to control, scale in the 19th century was attacked by sponging leaves or stems of affected plants with tobacco tea. We have done the same with soapy water, following this with a sponging of plain water.

The hellebore spray described under caterpillars was also used against scale on roses.

Another remedy for scale insects was: "Rub them off with a pine stick or something that will not injure the bark of the plant." Burlap is also a good thing to rub with, and we have used our fingers when dealing with tender plants such as some ferns.

Kerosene emulsions (see Aphids) was also used for scale.

SLUGS AND SNAILS

An old device to trap slugs and snails was: "Warm and wilt a cabbage leaf, put some grease on it and place it near the bush of

49

the slug at night. In the morning pick them off the leaf and kill or burn them. Wood ashes or coal ashes sprinkled on the plants is also a remedy."

Soot was once used as a slug repellent. In 1900 the Peter Henderson seed company offered imported Scotch soft coal soot at five cents a pound as "Of great value mixed in the soil near the surface to drive away slugs."

The white hellebore treatments described under caterpillars were also used against slugs.

Salt was sometimes used to kill slugs, and Johnson in 1851 mentioned the experience of an English farmer who spread about four or five bushels of common salt per acre for this purpose. He did this in the evening, and said that "in the morning each throw may be distinguished by the quantity of slime and the number of dead slugs lying on the ground. In some fields it has certainly been the means of preventing the destruction of the whole crop."

Lime was used in the same way, being dusted on the ground after dark.

Sow Bugs

Here is a tactic against sow and pill bugs, used in the 1880s: "I invert a flower pot in places where I have young things planted, then go around every two or three days with a pail of scalding water and destroy the hundreds of bugs which gather under these pots. They also attract slugs." Another gardener reported using the same technique with the addition of potato peelings and cabbage scraps under the pots as a lure. The following spring she reported that as of April 20, "I have not seen one." Some other gardeners warmed the cabbage leaves and rubbed them with lard for added attraction.

Striped Cucumber Beetle

The 1911 D. M. Ferry seed catalog advised for cucumbers: "Plant 15 to 20 seeds in a hill. After the plants begin to crowd and danger from the striped beetle is pretty well over, thin to three plants to the hill.

"The beetles may be kept off by a frequent dusting with air-slaked lime, soot or sifted ashes diluted with fine road earth. Care should be taken not to use too much of any of the above materials, for if used too freely they will kill the vines. The best protection against injury is a vigorous and rapid growth of the young plants."

Thrips

A strong solution of tobacco water as a spray, repeated for 10 or 12 days, was effective against thrips in his greenhouse, Peter Henderson reported in 1881. Kerosene emulsion (see Aphids) was also used against thrips.

Wireworms

From the 1870s comes this word on wireworms: "The wireworm and other insects may be trapped by means of potatoes cut in half, and the cut sides laid downwards. It is a good idea to trench all the vacant ground at this time of year [late summer]; grubs and wireworms are then buried deep enough to destroy them."

Set a Good Table with Yesterday's Garden

HERE are the garden plants that have supplied the American table for two centuries—and what a mouth-watering lot of them there are. Although most will be familiar friends to gardeners today, many will be surprises. In fact, if you'd like to grow what we might call a Yesterday's American Kitchen Garden, here are the plants to pick and choose among for that attractive experiment.

In assembling the listing, we decided it was better to omit any for which today's gardeners could no longer find seeds or plants. In spite of this limitation the list turned out to be surprisingly long; one of the early American garden writers, Bernard McMahon, noted many of them in his *American Gardener's Calendar*, first published in 1806 in Philadelphia. Gardeners of up to 200 years ago, we found, grew nearly every vegetable we grow today, even though in far fewer varieties, along with many other plants that are now hardly known. (By 1840, however, that ar-

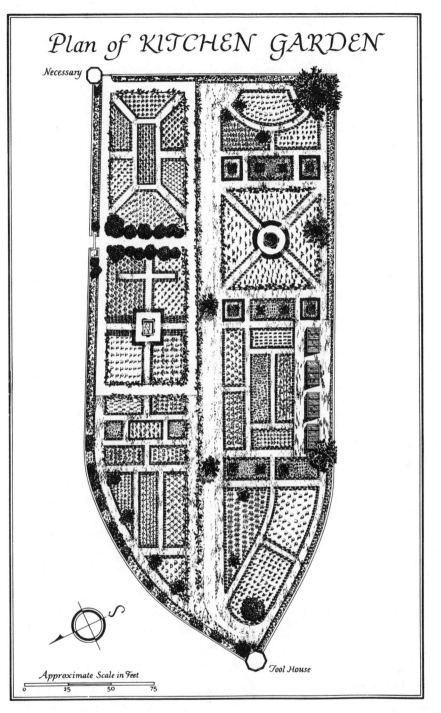

Plan of KITCHEN GARDEN

Necessary

Tool House

Approximate Scale in Feet

0 25 50 75

The spacious kitchen garden of Mount Vernon, George Washington's Virginia home, measured about 140' by 300'. It was laid out in symmetrical beds typical of colonial garden design, and produced vegetables, fruits, and herbs in abundance.

dent gardener, preacher Henry Ward Beecher, could plant, as he later reported in the *Western Farmer and Gardener*, 16 kinds of peas, 17 of beans, 7 of corn, 6 of squash, 8 of cabbage, 7 of lettuce, 8 of cucumber, and 7 of turnips.)

ARTICHOKE

That elegant perennial, the globe artichoke, dates back to at least the 16th century, being a form of a favorite of the ancients, the cardoon. The artichoke was not a plant favored by the New England or upper Midwest climates, but it was mentioned by McMahon as in America, and there were repeated references to it in the next few decades. Seeds were being offered at least as early as 1828. Later in the 19th century, seed catalogs commonly listed globe artichokes. Although happiest where summers are cool and often foggy, the plant was grown fairly widely, sometimes regarded as being as much an ornamental as a luxurious vegetable. In cold climates it was protected in winter with a heavy mulch after being cut to within a few inches of ground level.

Once started, an artichoke planting is good for at least three years, and can be continued indefinitely by transplanting suckers that arise from the roots of established plants. Globe artichokes are noted for demanding rich soil and frequent overhead watering. The edible buds, future flowers if allowed to mature, form where leaves and stalk meet, and in axils of stems themselves, and a hard-working plant may produce a dozen or more in a season.

How to eat an artichoke baffles many, so we give directions, from the 1850s and still sound: After the bud is boiled tender "the pod leaves are pulled off one at a time, dipped in butter, and the mealy part is stripped off by the teeth and the rest put aside. The bottom, when all leaves are thus disposed of is eaten with a knife and fork." This bottom is called the heart. Either before or after cooking, the choke, or undeveloped flower, should be cut out; it lies in the lower center of the bud.

Today globe artichoke seeds are offered by de Giorgi, Park, Shumway, and Thompson & Morgan.

ASPARAGUS

Although asparagus somehow seems modern, it was familiar to the Romans and came to America in colonial times. Yet even as late as 1880 a seedsman could complain that "this delicious vegetable is not as common in farmers' gardens as it should be." The same could have been said of household gardens and can be said today—which is a mystery, for asparagus is beautiful, a perennial, is not a demanding plant, and a bed will last for twenty years. Dig a 1'-deep trench and half-fill it with compost mixed with ¼ cup of bone meal per 1' of trench. Set roots 18" apart in the trench and gradually fill the trench with earth as the roots sprout. Asparagus does best where winters are not really mild, but will grow nearly anywhere in the United States.

Eighty years ago, incidentally, seedsman Joseph Harris was espousing an easier way to plant than the traditional deep trench. "We have a bed that was planted about ten years ago," he remarked, "that has furnished us an abundance of fine large asparagus every spring since the second year after it was started. There was hardly more work expended on this bed than in planting so many potatoes. All we did was to mark out the land in rows 3½ feet apart and plant the roots 2 feet apart in the rows and three or four inches deep. The bed contains about 400 plants and supplies a large family with all the asparagus they can desire, besides leaving some for the neighbors."

Asparagus takes three years before harvesting can begin, if started from seed, but this was a fairly common method in more leisurely times. If started from roots, it needs only two growing seasons prior to harvesting's starting.

It used to be the custom to sprinkle the bed with salt each spring, on the theory the plant's origin was the seacoast, but it was the manure gardeners spread on the bed each fall and again in the spring after cutting was over, that the plants thrived on. Today compost will perform this job—a 4" fall layer and a 2" spring one. A good established bed will yield for ten weeks each year, starting in mid-April.

ASPARAGUS CHICORY

Occasionally seen in 19th-century catalogs, this vegetable appears to be a chicory species, of which there are several. It is grown from spring-sown seed and given the same care as a leafy green, but the edible parts are the asparagus-like shoots that begin appearing in about ten weeks. Growth is vigorous and several harvests of shoots can be made during the season. The shoots are cooked like asparagus or can be used raw in salads. De Giorgi and Nichols list asparagus chicory.

Beans were one of the vegetables grown by early American gardeners, sometimes in varieties now crowded out by newer ones.

BEANS

Common beans and lima beans are native Americans. In fact, a bag of beans was waiting for the Pilgrims when they arrived in 1620, an Indian gift. There was a good deal of variation in appearance among what we are calling common beans here—as there is today—but they were botanically *Phaseolus vulgaris*, and included snap beans and kidney beans. Lima beans, *Phaseolus limensis*, were more seen in the southern colonies since the plants need a warm season. Beans are annual plants.

Another bean popular with early American gardeners was the broad bean or English bean, *Vicia faba*. It wants cool weather, as peas do, and is shelled out like a lima bean. It is usually listed today as the Fava bean. It tastes something like a pea.

Soybeans, *Glycine* genus, were unknown to early American gardeners, arriving in this country via the Perry Expedition to Japan, 1853-54, and were distributed in 1854 by the U.S. Patent Office (the Department of Agriculture not then existing). In the past few years more interest has been paid soybeans as a garden crop than before, but they are still a minor item, and seedmen seldom carry more than one variety, Kanrich being the one usually seen. Soybeans take a long warm summer, about 15 weeks.

The beans of the early colonists were pole types, and a device of the Indians was adopted—that of planting the beans with corn, so that the cornstalks formed the supporting poles for the beans. Later, for gardeners who preferred to keep their bean crop separate, the advice given by seedmen was to run the rows north and south, and set poles 3' apart and slanting slightly north. "Set in this way," it was stated, "the vines climb better, and the pods are straighter and more easily seen." Another 19th-century seedman advised planting pole beans in hills 4' apart and letting vines run on the ground.

Dug-in compost when seeding is ordinarily enough fertilizer for beans being grown in fertile soil. If growth is slow, side-dress young plants with ½ pound of cottonseed meal to 30' of row. Lima beans should not be seeded until weather is warm, but the others can be seeded in the spring, and for these, some old advice ran: "If there is danger of frost just as the beans are cracking the earth, draw a little light soil over them with the hoe."

Among the blessings of beans to early American gardeners was their ease of drying, good keeping qualities, and compactness for storage.

BEETS

Beets were known to ancient civilizations in the Mediterranean area, but the beet as a garden vegetable was not prominent for a long time, making a slow beginning in about the 14th century in

England and France, though some say later. By colonial times in America beets were no rarity, although there was little choice in varieties—one or two red beets being the only ones available— and by 1821 William Cobbett could say that beets were in as common use here as carrots were in England. Beets are grown as annuals.

An early-19th-century seed catalog listed four varieties of beets, and this grew until by the 1880s at least a dozen were offered, in various shapes and for various seasons, and in white and yellow as well as red roots.

Work compost generously into the soil before seeding beets. Mulch with compost when half grown, and keep the planting well watered. Old practice, if very early beets were wanted, was to sow seed in hotbeds and transplant seedlings later to the garden after removing the outer leaves. As this suggests, beet thinnings in the garden can also be transplanted.

BELGIAN ENDIVE
(SEE CHICORY)

BROCCOLI

Broccoli as most of us know it ("sprouting broccoli"), was a stranger to American gardens until at least the first half of the 18th century. And even though it became known well enough so that four varieties were being grown by the end of that century, gardeners were still also calling it cauliflower-broccoli, sprout-cauliflower, and sometimes Italian asparagus. In fact it took broccoli until the 1930s to really catch on with the American public.

For early broccoli, plant seeds indoors in early spring and move to compost-enriched soil in late March. For a late crop, seed in the garden in mid-summer. Give a side-dressing of compost when plants are half grown. Broccoli is treated as an annual.

After you harvest the central sprout, side sprouts will give you a second crop over the next several weeks.

BRUSSELS SPROUTS

With broccoli, Brussels sprouts constitute the upper class of the cabbage family. The sprouts are cabbages in miniature, borne in the angle each of the leaf stems makes with the central stalk. The harvest can be exceedingly generous, and we have had single plants produce about a hundred sprouts.

Brussels sprouts were known to some American gardeners in the late-18th century, but the plant was not at all well known— nor is it today. Most seed houses offer only one or two varieties, usually including the good hybrid Jade Cross. The widest selection we know of is handled by Stokes, which offers eight; Thompson & Morgan offers six. The "Brussels" in the name of this vegetable is for Brussels, Belgium, where it was first grown as a major crop.

A good feature of Brussels sprouts is their indifference to freezing weather. Like kale, sprouts gain in flavor from a freeze, and will go through a northern winter with a straw mulch. Grow them as annuals.

To get the best growth, plant seed in May, transplant to the garden in compost-enriched soil about six weeks later; in mid-September, when lower sprouts are nearing harvestable (1"-wide) size, pinch out the plant's growing tip at the top. This throws strength into sprout development. Harvest lowest sprouts first, breaking off the leaf under each as you harvest it.

BURDOCK

This plant, usually regarded as a weed, and bearing burs, has an edible root and was being eaten in pre-Revolutionary times in parts of New England. We suspect it was wild rather than in gardens, but are including it for historical interest. An 1847 English writer, Anne Pratt, said in her book *The Field, The Garden, and The Woodland*, that burdock was "eaten either as a salad or a boiled vegetable; and the young stalks are said when cooked to have the flavour of asparagus." Gobo is the name burdock is likely to be called when found at all in modern seed catalogs, and its botanical name is *Arctium lappa*. Roots are long (up to 2′) and slender, and are prepared by washing, scraping, and boiling until tender. It is grown as an annual from seed, much like carrots, and is listed by Gurney, Johnny, Kitazawa, and Nichols.

BURNET

Not easily found today, burnet was once grown in some American gardens for salads, as its young leaves taste like cucumbers. "It is a perennial, and a very poor thing," Cobbett observed impatiently. If this doesn't discourage you, you can start burnet from seed and continue thereafter by dividing and replanting roots in the spring. The plant takes little care, preferring poor soil and not even needing much water. If your soil is acid, work in some wood ashes before planting. Height is 18″, and plants bear attractive white or red flowers. Nichols and Park carry the seeds, among herbs.

Cabbage was so popular with earlier American gardeners, seedsmen regularly offered dozens of varieties; this one was called Marbled Burgundy Drumhead.

CABBAGE

This ancient and popular plant was grown by early American colonists, as might be expected, and was in fact so taken for granted as a garden vegetable, not much mention is found of it. Cabbages were growing in Virginia as early as 1669, and there was a good choice of early and late varieties by the end of the next century if not well before that. There is a good choice today, twenty being not unusual although this is half the number of varieties offered some sixty years ago by many seedsmen. Today in home gardens the small cabbage is popular, and there are even some midget cabbages of baseball size or smaller, weighing about 8 ounces. Years ago it was the big cabbage that got the attention, such as one a West Virginia customer of Peter Henderson's reported raising in 1899: "I this day measured what we think is our largest and it is just 47 inches around, clean solid goods, and weighs 26 pounds."

Cabbage is a cool-weather crop, taking up to three months to mature. Plants are often started indoors in February for the early crop, and seed can be sown in the garden in July for the fall crop. Dig compost generously into the bed beforehand, and side dress half-grown plants with ½ cup of cottonseed meal per plant.

CANTALOUPES

The delicious cantaloupe, variously known as muskmelon, pepone, pompion, and so on, seems to have originated in the Old World tropics, and dates its present form from about the 15th century. The plant was certainly grown in America by early settlers, and was popular with the Indian tribes who knew and planted it and who quickly distributed it about the country.

Cantaloupes have continued their constant popularity with American home gardeners ever since, and became a substitute source of molasses and sugar in the South during the Civil War, as these sweet fruits can be cooked down for syrup.

Nineteenth-century seedsmen sometimes offered a surprisingly wide choice of cantaloupes; we counted 22 in one catalog, 15 in another. The Bay View was a popular old variety, introduced in 1877, a 10-pound melon that could reach 20 pounds if given tender loving care and plenty of fertilizing. Another

61

melon, Montreal Green Nutmeg, was recorded as having reached nearly 40 pounds, at least for one record-breaking whopper.

Plant cantaloupes in soil well enriched with dug-in compost, and give them three warm months from seeding to serving. A unique characteristic of cantaloupes is their readiness to part from the stem when ripe, a sure way to time the harvest.

CARAWAY

Found exclusively among the herbs in seed catalogs today, caraway in earlier times was also grown as a vegetable, and many an 18th-century American gardener raised caraway solely for the sake of its leaves and roots; the delicately flavored roots were cooked like carrots, and the ferny leaves eaten in salads or cooked as greens or put into soups.

The plant is one of the old ones, dating back beyond recorded history to the ancient lake dwellings of what is now Switzerland. It is a biennial, the seeds coming the second year, though sometimes the first one if seeding is quite early.

CARDOON

This relative of the globe artichoke is grown for its leaf stalks—just as celery is—except that after blanching, cardoon stalks are most often cooked; the flavor is good but somewhat bitter. Cardoon was a favorite with ancient Romans and esteemed by many peoples through the centuries, though more in the south of Europe than the north. English gardeners grew it infrequently, and in young America the plant was seen in only an occasional garden. The old catalogs, when they listed cardoon, recommended it for salads and soups, and for cooking like asparagus.

To grow this old vegetable, sow its seeds early in spring, in a coldframe or indoors, and move plants to the garden in late spring. Thereafter the cardoon will come up year after year. Like the globe artichoke, it requires winter protection in cold climates, and in fact its culture is the same as the artichoke's.

The best way to blanch the leaf stalks is to tie a paper band

62

around them when plants have made a good growth. Cardoon seed is listed by de Giorgi, le Jardin, and Nichols.

CARROTS

Introduced into England by the Dutch in Elizabeth I's reign, the carrot was a staple in American gardens from the beginning, a must in soups and stews. Also, grown as a field crop, it provided good winter feed for cattle, horses, sheep, and pigs. Although it has never been first in popularity among American vegetable lovers and has not achieved the bon vivant standing it has long had in France, an interesting point about the carrot is that there is as good or better a range of varieties offered today as was offered a century ago—something that cannot be said of every vegetable. Danvers and Chantenay are still with us as leading varieties, and in addition there are some good hybrid carrots now available and some new midget carrots. Grow carrots as annuals.

Spread 4" of compost and dig it in well before sowing carrots. By not seeding thickly you can save seed and avoid much tiresome thinning. As an old seedsman put it, "They can be left in bunches of four or five together. They will crowd each other like a bunch of onions, and if the soil is rich enough and the weeds are kept out you will have a great yield."

CAULIFLOWER

The histories of broccoli and cauliflower are mingled, and it appears most probably that broccoli came first, with cauliflower appearing later as a result of continued selection of the type of broccoli called heading broccoli. American gardens had cauliflower in them in the 18th century, and in several varieties. The plant is not as willing a grower as broccoli but has always been prized. It likes very rich soil, cool weather, and dampness. "Hoe frequently and suffer not a weed to grow," warned an old seedsman. Cauliflower is an annual, and a late crop is more apt to succeed than an early one. Seed in May and transplant to 2' apart in rich soil by or before July 1. When the head starts to form, tie

63

the inner leaves together over it, for blanching. Well grown, a cauliflower can be immense. "Some weighed as high as 28 pounds," a customer wrote seedsman W. Atlee Burpee in 1900.

CELERIAC

This near relative of celery, grown for its large root, was in American gardens in the early 1800s but probably not in the early colonial gardens. Even today celeriac is not widely known or grown despite consistent listing by seedsmen all through the years —even by one who in his 1880 catalog complained: "I either do not know how to raise this variety or it is not worthy of much attention; it is useful, perhaps, for flavoring soup, etc."

Celeriac is grown as an annual, and takes the same care as celery.

CELERY

As a cultivated food plant, celery —once considered strictly a medicine—dates back only to the 17th century in Europe and was something of a luxury. A century later it was becoming better known, was popular in soups, and was definitely in American gardens by the end of the 18th century. Cobbett in 1821 speaks of white celery, red celery, hollow celery, and solid celery.

An old term for celery was "smallage" or "smellage," and this little incident concerning it occurred about 1870. A customer asked for seeds of "smellage" at a New York City seed store, to the bafflement of the clerks. A woman customer spoke up, saying, "My grandmother's mother had it in her garden, and always used to chew a piece on Sunday before she went to church, to make her breath sweet." The other customer answered, "That's what my wife wants it for," and the woman told him: "You will have to ask for it by another name. They call it celery nowadays, but in old times they did not know it was fit to eat for a vegetable."

The old catalogs were explicit about the culture of celery. They warned that seed is slow to sprout, and the seed bed must be kept moist, "almost wet," said one. Seedlings were transplant-

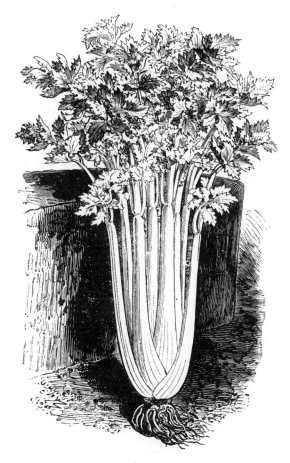

Celery has been a garden favorite for years. This plant is shown as if in a trench, ready to be surrounded with earth for blanching.

Celery was often bleached by standing boards on each side of the row to exclude light.

65

ed twice to grow sturdy roots. We dig 4″ of compost into the seed bed and mulch half grown plants with compost. A side dressing of cottonseed meal at this time, a pound to 20′ of row, is helpful. Like many biennials, celery is grown as an annual.

Blanching was nearly always done in years past, and was called "handling." The plant was held together with one hand while the other drew earth around it. An experienced gardener seldom made the error of letting any earth sift into the interior of the plant as this would cause discoloring or rotting.

Related to the beet, chard is an old vegetable, long popular for its well-flavored leaves, used as cooking greens; the handsome white leaf stalks are also cooked.

CHARD

Botanically almost identical with the beet, chard is an ancient vegetable that was known to Aristotle. But although it seems a logical plant to have been in colonial gardens of America, we have found no mention of it until the middle of the 19th century. Old seed catalogs paid chard scant attention, dropping in a reference to it at the end of the beets, if at all. It was ordinarily called Swiss chard, sometimes silver beet, and had a name for being a variable plant that sometimes grew peculiar-looking specimens from an occasional seed, which is still the case, to a mild degree. A catalog of the 1880s listed chard as follows: "Sown early in the spring it makes a rapid growth of leaves and is fit for use for greens sooner than any other variety [of beet]. Later the leaves grow very large, with broad, flat, beautifully white and wax-like stems and mid-ribs, which are cooked like asparagus, or made into most attractive pickles. It also furnishes admirable and healthy food for chickens."

Chard takes about the same care as beets, and like them is grown as an annual. It should be added that one of the good points about chard is an ability to grow in hot weather without bolting to seed nearly as quickly as does spinach. But here again, the plants are variable, and we have had half of a bed of a dozen or so chard plants hold firm through a hot spell while their comrades called it a day and arranged to go to seed.

CHAYOTE

American gardeners in the warmest areas of the South, Southwest, and West have grown this squash-like vegetable for many years. There, chayote is a perennial and prolific, a single vine producing up to 100 fruits in a season. They average close to a pound each. Related to squashes, the chayote looks something like a big, deeply furrowed, light-green pear. It is cooked like a summer squash, and is rather bland. We first knew chayote as mirliton, its name in Louisiana and Mississippi. The single seed also is edible when boiled, and the tuberous roots can be cooked like potatoes.

Chayote wants rich soil, full sun, and plenty of water, and it is best to plant three or more vines to insure good pollination. Space them 10' apart and give trellis support. We know of no source for seed, but if you live in chayote-growing territory you can plant the chayote you find in the supermarket. Plant the whole fruit, letting the stem end stick out of the soil an inch or so.

CHICORY

By "chicory" is meant an endive grown mainly for its root. The root is then sprouted during the winter. Botanically this chicory is *Cichorium intybus* and is listed today by seed houses as witloof chicory. The name used today for the winter sprouts is French or Belgian endive, but old catalogs called them by their European name, as in this description from a Burpee listing in the middle 1880s: "This variety produces the '*Barbe de Capucin*,' a salad much used in France."

This chicory is an old plant, also familiar in the Orient, and makes itself so at home that it becomes a perennial weed seen on roadsides in summer, its pretty little daisy-like blue flowers a cheerful sight. Sow seed in June and care for the plants as you do lettuce.

We do not know when the first chicory was seeded in America, but its multiple use would have recommended it to early settlers, for the leaves can be cropped, moderately, for greens while the root is growing, and the root can be cooked and eaten like a carrot or made into a coffee substitute (see Chapter 7), as well as used for forcing the winter sprouts—done by planting the roots in a keg in the basement and covering them with 8" of sand or sawdust.

CHINESE CABBAGE

This annual plant was unknown to the first American gardeners, for it did not even reach Europe from the Orient until 1837. Introduced into the U.S. in 1885, it caught on slowly, and only an occasional later 19th-century and early 20th-century seed catalog listed Chinese cabbage. It became known as celery cabbage, not for any celery flavor but because the heading type, the pe-tsai, roughly resembles celery's growth habit. There is another Chinese cabbage type, pak-choy, that grows more as chard does, and is harvested the same way, a leaf at a time rather than taking the whole plant at once.

This Chinese cabbage is of the non-heading type called pak-choy, harvested a leaf at a time like chard.

Chinese cabbage usually does best as a fall crop. Plant seed in the garden in July in compost-enriched soil and thin plants to 8″ apart. It is apt to bolt if transplanted—thus the seeding directly in the garden where plants will remain.

CHUFA

American gardeners of the mid-19th century grew this nut-like plant, although never to a great extent, and it has remained a garden curiosity. Other names for it are earth almond, garden almond, and Zulu nut. The fact it has survived is an indication of basic worth, and indeed this little delicacy has been around for so long that its tubers have been found in Egyptian tombs dating back more than 2000 years before Christ.

Like the peanut, the chufa grows its nuts underground; they are white and can be roasted like peanuts (30 minutes in a 300° F. oven), or eaten raw. They remind some people of coconut, and are sweet and good. They mature early in the fall and can be left in the ground until wanted. Another merit of the chufa is, it is a perennial, so that one planting does the job. Given a chance, it may acclimate itself to grow wild as do chicory and Jerusalem artichokes.

The 1881 Ferry catalog described the tubers as "about ¾″ long by 3/8″ through, tender, sweet, not unlike a chestnut though much sweeter." It was advised to soak the tubers in water for eight or ten days before planting them, changing the water every two or three days. In the North the tubers are planted in April or May when weather has turned warm. Seed in hills, two or three tubers per hill, covering with 1″ of earth and spacing hills 15″ apart.

Chufa tubers are hard to find today, but Gurney lists them. The plant's botanical name is *Cyperus esculentus.*

CITRON

This plant is a watermelon grown solely for making preserves. "A clear, transparent preserve of peculiar fine flavor," was the description in a seed catalog of 50 years ago. (The citron that is found in candied form for use in fruitcakes is from a different plant.)

Citron was almost always listed by 19th-century seedsmen and is still listed by some today. Fruits are about the size of a cantaloupe, with hard white flesh. Citron is grown as watermelons are grown, and is an annual. Seed is carried by Farmer, Field, Gurney, Olds, Shumway, and Stokes.

CLARY

This is a herb that was considered a vegetable by early gardeners. It is related to sage, being botanically *Salvia sclarea.* Leaves of clary were cooked, or went raw into salads. The flowers made a potent wine and can also make a tea. The plant is a biennial, like parsley. Sow seeds in spring and move seedlings to the garden in a fairly dry spot. Height is about 3′ and the bluish-white flowers are borne in attractive racemes. Nichols lists clary seed, among herbs.

COLLARDS

Although collards have always been associated with gardens in the South, they are, like the other cabbage-group plants, a cool-weather crop, but will take more heat than the others. They were a minor item in seed catalogs of the 1880s and later—as they are today—but were certainly being planted by American gardeners years before this, and are an old annual vegetable. Cultivation is the same as for kale. Collards are one of the most nutritious crops grown. The parts eaten are the leaves, pulled while still tender. They grow along the upright stem, with a terminal tuft at the top.

COMFREY

Ordinarily comfrey is and was found in the herb garden when found at all, but some 19th-century housewives raised it as a food plant also. Its young leaves were cooked like mustard or turnip greens, stalks were blanched like celery and cooked like chard stalks or asparagus, and the tuberous roots were peeled and steamed or boiled, something like potatoes, or were included in vegetable soups.

Plants grow 3' or 4' tall and are perennial and hardy. They can be grown from seeds or from root divisions, the latter being listed by Gurney, Hemlock Hill, and Nichols.

CORN

Corn is an ancient native American vegetable, which Columbus discovered in 1492 in Cuba, says Dr. E. Lewis Sturtevant in *Sturtevant's Edible Plants of the World*. When North America began to be settled by Europeans, corn, obtained from Indians, was among the early crops grown. Most of the corn the Indians were growing was like our field corn today—intended to be let mature on the stalk and then gathered when dry, for winter storage. Sweet corn, for eating fresh, was also grown by Indians, but few colonial gardeners knew sweet corn until about the time of the Revolutionary War, and it took another fifty years or more for it to start becoming somewhat familiar in household gardens. By the 1880s seedsmen were offering up to about 20 varieties, calling it "sweet," "sugar," or "table" corn, and popcorn also appeared in the listings. At this time, white corn was outnumbering yellow by five to one. Today in a typical listing, yellow sweet corn will outnumber white by two to one or more.

To grow corn you need about three months of warm

This wood engraving of ears of sweet corn appeared in some old seed catalogs.

weather, although some fast varieties mature nine weeks after seeding. Plant seed in late spring in fertile soil enriched with compost. Pick an open site and plant in blocks rather than in rows—say 4 to 6 rows about 30″ apart, with a corn plant every 12″ in each row. Ears are ripe when the silks are dry; harvest them within two or three days afterward, and only minutes before you are ready to cook them.

CORN SALAD

Botanically *Valerianella locusta olitoria*, this annual plant is also called lamb's lettuce, fetticus, and vettikost. Its leaves are eaten raw in salads and are cooked as greens. It probably entered gardens in the 16th century after growing wild in Europe, and was well known in American gardens in the 1700s if not sooner. Seeds are sown in compost-enriched soil from mid-spring through the summer, since the plant tolerates hot weather well (and will also winter over, given a light mulch). It grows to about 12" tall, doing so in 4 to 6 weeks in summer. It has never been an important item in seedmen's catalogs, and not every one carries it today. Five that do are de Giorgi, Harris, le Jardin, Shumway, and Stokes.

CRESS

This quick-growing little salad plant was well known to the first American gardeners. The cress we mean is garden cress or peppergrass, once also called tongue-grass, botanically *Lepidium sativa*. It is an annual plant, usually available in both curled-leaf and flat-leaf varieties. (There is a perennial plant called upland cress, *Barbarea* being its generic name; it has been grown to a very limited extent in American gardens; de Giorgi, Nichols, and Shumway list it.)

Garden cress is a cool-weather crop, growing to usable size (4" to 6" high) in a month, when you can begin snipping off parts of the tops. It then lasts for another month, although we have found that a late fall seeding in a mild climate can last into the winter. The curled variety is the more attractive, deserving to be better known. In fact, few gardeners of our acquaintance grow cress or have even heard of it, although it has been known since pre-Christian times. It is thought to have originated in Persia. There is also a yellow-leaved cress but we know of no source for seeds. Houses carrying plain or curled cress include Burpee, de Giorgi, Gurney, Harris, Nichols, Olds, Shumway, and Stokes.

CUCUMBERS

These are among the old, old vegetables, probably of Asian origin, and grown in American gardens by the early colonists, who knew them as "cowcumbers." Even before that, Columbus planted cucumbers at Haiti in 1494. The fruits were so popular, cultivation of cucumbers spread northward to Canada where, some 40 years later, Indians were found growing them in large quantities.

Cucumbers have always been a staple annual of home gardens, and part of their appeal was and is their value for pickling —an important method of preserving food, especially several generations ago.

Cucumbers are grown in the way cantaloupes are, needing rich soil and a warm season for best results. Something to keep in mind about harvesting cucumbers is that you must keep them picked to keep them bearing. As old seedsman Joseph Harris put it in 1880: "The sooner you cut the cucumbers the less will the vines be exhausted. If you allow even one cucumber to go to seed it will greatly reduce the productiveness of the vines."

CURRANTS

Until the 16th century the currant was a wild fruit. Domestication of this perennial made the berries larger and less seedy, and some of these new plants were being grown in Massachusetts as early as in the 1630s. Since currants want a moist, cool climate, they were never grown widely in this country, although they will provide some sort of a crop almost anywhere but in the hottest and driest regions.

Fall planting is best, with plenty of compost dug in. Thereafter a mulch of compost mixed with straw should be kept on the bed. A good spacing is 5' between plants.

Red currants are the ones usually listed, and are the most popular, with white kinds next; black currants are seldom available. N.Y. Co-op and Southmeadow list White Imperial. They and these others list red currants: Field, Gurney, Miller, and Shumway.

DANDELIONS

It is fairly certain that although the early colonists in America ate dandelion leaves and roots, it was the wild plant they used. The dandelion, a perennial, did not move into the household garden until after the Civil War. Speaking of it in 1821 as a wildling, Cobbett called it "A most wicked garden weed," and said,

So willing a grower that it is a weed in lawns, the dandelion is also a nutritious and multi-purpose garden plant, well worth cultivating.

"I am half afraid to speak of using it as food, lest I should encourage laziness," but he brought himself to recommend it to those of the poor who had no gardens.

The plant was listed in catalogs beginning in the 1870s. Seed is sown in May or June. Leaves are put in salads or are cooked. Roots can also be harvested, and the dandelion is so persistent in growth, it will survive even this if a bit of root is left in the earth. Given a choice, dandelions prefer rich soil and sun, but will grow anywhere. The root was listed in old materia medicas as a source of extracts used for treating liver ailments and some other problems. (See Chapter 7 for employment of the plant in beverages.) Dandelion seed is carried by Burpee, Johnny, Nichols, Shumway, and Thompson & Morgan.

EGGPLANT

A native of the Old World tropics, according to Sturtevant, the eggplant was not an ancient vegetable in Europe, but was well enough established there in the 16th century to be among the annuals brought to America for household-garden cultivation. Fruits of these early eggplants were probably smaller than the largest

75

kinds grown today, and were white and yellow as well as the familiar purple. Color variation is available today also: white eggplants are listed by Farmer, Nichols, Park, and Shumway; yellow ones by Gurney and Nichols; and a green one by Farmer.

Old seedsmen sometimes credited eggplants with more nutrition than they possess, perhaps because they sounded and looked the part. At any rate, this vegetable has been a home garden favorite in a modest way for many years. It takes a long warm season to do well, and the advice of the 19th-century New York State seedsman Joseph Harris is valid today: "There is no difficulty in raising this delicious vegetable in the open air, after you have got the plants. But the plants must be raised in a hotbed or in boxes in the house. Sow the seed in this latitude the first or second week in April; set out the plants in the garden the first or second week of June, in a loose, warm soil. . . . Select a warm, sheltered situation, and keep the ground mellow and free from weeds. Hill up a little as the plants grow, and keep off the potato bugs." We would add only: Dig compost into the planting spots generously before moving seedlings to the garden, and use compost as a hilled-up mulch when plants are half grown.

ENDIVE

Here is another very old plant, known to the early Egyptians and to the Greeks and Romans, who enjoyed it as a salad and also in cooked form. Endive probably arrived in America with some of the early colonists. The broad-leaf and curled-leaf kinds were being grown in the 18th century. The broad-leaf one, now identified by the name Batavian endive, or escarole, appears to be the endive known to the ancients.

You grow endive as an annual, much as you do lettuce. It is an excellent plant for fall cooking greens, and if seeded in late fall will provide early greens the following spring. It also can be carried over during the winter by protecting half-grown plants with a coldframe. Endive is often blanched, and used raw for salads this produces attractive and milder leaves. An old method was to place a slate, or a flower pot upside down, over the center of the plant, rather than tying the outside leaves together over the plant's top. The danger in leaf-tying is that rot may destroy the plant if much moisture is thus trapped inside.

A beautiful ferney plant, Florence fennel is well worth growing for its anise-flavored, succulent, bulb-like base.

FLORENCE FENNEL   Also known as finochio, anise, and celery-rooted fennel, this plant was in some American gardens in the 19th century, but was not at all widely known either here or in England. It is not widely known to-day either, but is worth a try by any gardener, to see if he likes its anise-like taste. ("A rather peculiar but delightful flavor," one old seedsman wrote.) We acquired a taste for it after not caring much about it, and are glad we persisted. Grow it as an annual, seeding it in the spring, and thinning plants to 6" apart in rows 30" apart.

Old catalogs tended to ignore Florence fennel, although they often carried its close relative, sweet fennel, grown as a culinary and medical herb for many centuries. Today you are likely as not to find Florence fennel also listed among herbs in seed catalogs.

Its large ferny leaves can be used as a flavoring but the enlarged base of the plant just above ground level is what you primarily grow this vegetable for. Quarter it, steam it tender, and finish cooking it in butter.

FRENCH ENDIVE
(SEE CHICORY)

GARLIC

Garlic, an ancient Asian plant, was grown in colonial gardens and seems to have been introduced into the New World in the 16th century. (A curious old antidote for garlic breath was to finish off by eating a raw stringbean, chewing it well.) Garlic has continued to be an American garden plant, easily grown from the segments, called cloves, that form the bulbs. Set them in early spring, 2" deep and 6" apart, with pointed tips up, and give them four months to mature, treating them as annuals. If you run short of bulbs for flavoring, you can snip off a little garlic leaf, and can even grow garlic for this purpose on the kitchen window-sill in winter.

GOOSEBERRIES

This bush fruit has never been as wildly popular in America as in parts of England, but was known to early settlers in the wild forms, and by at least the early 19th century, cultivated varieties were in some American gardens north of Philadelphia. The fruit was a minor item in old catalogs we have examined. Indeed, it is a minor item today with all but one house, Southmeadow, which lists an astonishing total of sixteen varieties. Others handling gooseberries include Burgess, Farmer, Field, Gurney, Miller, N.Y. Co-op, and Shumway.

Gooseberries do their best where summers are not awfully hot, and they like a moist and shady spot. Plant the bushes in the spring, working a good bushel of compost into each site, and space them 8' apart. Once planted, a gooseberry bed is good for about 20 years.

GROUND CHERRY

This "curious little fruit," as an old seedsman called it, was being grown in 19th-century American gardens for the sake of its small yellow berries that were made into preserves and pies. "They are also excellent to eat raw as fruit," an old catalog stated. The fruits are enclosed in papery husks, and "husk tomato" is another name for the plant, a hardy annual which belongs to the Physalis genus and is related to the true tomatoes. The fruits keep well if stored in the husks until wanted.

The plant settled into the status of a garden curiosity years ago, but has continued to be offered by some seed houses. Among them today are Burgess, de Giorgi, Farmer, Field, Olds, and Shumway.

The plants need about three months to produce, so seed them indoors and move to the garden when frost is over, like tomatoes. Growth is low and vining.

HOPS

Although thought of almost exclusively as one of the ingredients used in beer making (for which female blossoms supply the hop, or fruit), hops were once also a kitchen-garden herb, and were so used by some early American gardeners. Hops also grew wild in some parts of the country. The young shoots were cut before they produced leaves, and were included in salads. Hops were also used in yeast (see Chapter 7).

The plant is a tall perennial that produces male and female flowers on separate plants, and can become a pesky weed if it escapes. It is propagated by planting 4"-long roots, set with buds pointing upward, and ½" below ground level. A source of the roots is the May Nursery, Yakima, Washington 98907.

HORSERADISH

Known in Europe from early times, horseradish was being grown in American gardens in the 18th century. It had no great following in England, although it was grown there enough for William Cobbett to say in 1821 that an 8' by 16' bed of it would "produce enough for a family that eats roast-beef every day of their lives." Horseradish was popular in Germany in those days and before, where it was used as an accompaniment to meat after being sliced thinly and steeped in vinegar.

Horseradish is one of the garden's perennial vegetables, but for best results the bed should be moved every two or three years. To start a new bed, spade in compost and plant, 2" deep, finger-length sections of the small roots that grow from the sides of the large ones you harvest for grating into sauce. These are also the roots sold by seedsmen. Horseradish grows best where winters are not mild.

An interesting variation in planting, treating horseradish as an annual crop, was given by the old seedsman W. Atlee Burpee in 1896: "To economize when land is limited, the roots are planted in May between early cabbages. Holes are made from 8 to 10 inches deep; plant the roots at least 3 inches below the surface. The deep planting is to retard growth until the cabbage is removed. The root makes its chief growth after midsummer and during autumn."

JERUSALEM
ARTICHOKES

Here we have another native American vegetable. Several Indian tribes knew and raised it or sought it out as an edible wild plant. As such, it was known in Massachusetts by 1605 and was soon domesticated. The plant is a perennial that dies back to the ground each fall, so was able to take the New England winters, while flourishing as well in milder American climates.

The edible parts are the tubers, which can be cooked like potatoes. They are harvested in late fall. The tops look like sunflower plants, for the Jerusalem artichoke is a close relative of the sunflower and has nothing whatever to do with either Jerusalem or artichokes.

Curiously, Jerusalem artichokes have never been widely planted in American gardens despite the plant's merits, which include excellent productivity and small care. Simply plant tubers

4″ deep and 2′ apart. In fact, according to Cobbett, the plant takes so little care, "a handful of its roots, flung about a piece of ground of any sort, will keeep bearing forever, in spite of grass and of weeds."

For a while, by the 1860s, Jerusalem artichokes seemed to be going somewhere, with four different varieties isolated (each having a different color of skin—white, red, purple, and yellow), but today only the white-skinned one is commonly known. Few seed catalogs listed Jerusalem artichokes years ago, and gardeners must have obtained tubers from other gardeners growing the plant, or by digging up those found growing wild. Today you can get tubers to start your own planting, from Burgess, Gurney, le Jardin, Nichols, Park, or Thompson & Morgan.

KALE

This is another ancient plant—at least in some forms that may not have looked exactly like today's kales. Kale was mentioned as growing in Virginia in 1669, and for years the spelling was "cale." Another name for kale is borecole, meaning, in the original Dutch, peasant cabbage. Kale's willingness to grow along through winter cold, however, suggests it was grown earlier than 1669 in American gardens. Although never approaching the popularity of cabbage, kale has continued to be a home garden familiar through the centuries in this country. It is grown as an annual.

Seed kale in late summer in rich soil, thin to 6″ apart, and side dress with compost. The plants will provide greens all fall and winter. Harvest outer leaves, and others continue to form.

KOHLRABI

This cabbage-family vegetable was grown in some 18th-century American gardens, but it appears to have been infrequently planted even though it was known in Europe dating back to the 16th century. A good reason for this infrequency, we would guess, is that some other vegetables make more efficient use of the garden space. However, most 19th-century seed catalogs listed at least

81

one variety of kohlrabi (advising the gardeners that the crop would be relished by livestock, in case the family didn't care for it), and it is listed today, in white-skinned and purple-skinned varieties. Although sometimes classed as a root crop, kohlrabi grows its bulb—the edible part of the plant—just above ground level. It is an annual, and for an early crop, seen in flats in mid-February and set plants out 4 to 6 weeks later in compost-enriched soil. Side dress with cottonseed meal when half grown. The fall crop can be seeded in the garden 2 months before cold weather is due.

LEEKS

Leeks were also grown in early American gardens, three varieties being mentioned by McMahon. One merit of this annual

Leeks hold a place as distinguished members of the onion group, taking a long time to grow, and requiring blanching, but repaying the trouble with their fine eating qualities.

plant for the early settlers was its willingness to remain in the ground until wanted, needing no more than a light covering of straw in the coldest winter climates. Though considered a minor vegetable, the leek has been offered by most seed catalogs through the years, and in more varieties at times than at present. Stokes offers a choice of four, however.

Seed leeks in compost-enriched ground, thin them to 6" apart later, transplanting the thinnings. Give them 4 months to mature, and side dress when half grown with a pound of cottonseed meal to 20' of row. Cobbett's recommendation was: "Hoe deeply and frequently till the middle of July and then take the plants up, cut their roots off to an inch long, and cut off the leaves also a good way down. Make trenches, like those for celery, only not more than half as deep, and half as wide apart. [He called for 12"-deep trenches for celery, 5' apart.] Manure the trenches with rotten dung or other rich manure. Put in the plants about five inches asunder. As the leeks grow, earth them up by degrees like celery; and at last you will have leeks 18 inches long underground, and as thick as your wrist."

LETTUCE

Lettuce has been the king of annual salad plants for so long that its beginnings—in Europe or the Orient, or both—are lost in the mists of the centuries. No wonder, then, that the first American gardeners knew and grew this plant for the salads they loved, and soon grew it in great variety, for by the end of the 18th century well over a dozen kinds of lettuces were being grown in America. By the 1880s a seedsman was able to say, "The varieties of lettuce are innumerable." In those days the heading type of lettuce was often called "cabbage lettuce," and this reference continued to be used by gardeners for years.

Some of the old cabbage lettuces were Tennis Ball, Red Besson (its leaves tinged with red), American Gathering, and Black-Seeded Satisfaction. The other class of lettuce distinguished by old seedsmen was the cos, or romaine. It is still popular, and today the other lettuces are divived into three classes: crisp-heads such as Iceberg, butterheads such as Bibb, and looseheads such as Salad Bowl.

Lettuce is traditionally a cool-weather crop, and this applies most specifically to all but loosehead kinds, which can be grown fairly well in summer heat if given partial shade, plenty of water, and a soil rich in organic matter. All lettuces, in fact, demand organic matter if they are to do well. An old seed catalog carried this caution regarding lettuces: "Hoe frequently to prevent them from going to seed."

LOVAGE

Here is another herb that appears to have been used as a vegetable by some early American gardeners, in the way it had been used in the Europe they had left behind them. The plant somewhat resembles celery, and the leaf stalks can be eaten raw like celery. The flavor is described as sweet and aromatic. Lovage is an old herb, known to the ancients, and is native to Europe.

A perennial, it can be started by sowing seed in summer, then transplanting plants the following spring. Thereafter, you can dig and replant roots each spring to increase the planting. We know of four sources of seed today: Johnny, le Jardin, Nichols, and Park.

MARTYNIA

The seed pods of this native American plant, also called the unicorn plant, were pickled by 19th-century American gardeners, who also grew martynia for its showy white, yellow, and violet flowers. The plant is an annual, the seeds started early and transplanted after frost for a long bearing season. Space plants 3' apart, in rich soil. The green fuzzy seed pods are gathered as soon as they are half grown, when the plant is about 2 months old, if wanted for pickling. When allowed to mature, the pods can be used as decorations (covered in Chapter 7). De Giorgi, Park, and Shumway list martynia.

MUSTARD

Mustard was being grown in colonial gardens by at least the end of the 18th century. Both black mustard and white mustard (most easily identified by seed color) were grown, both yielding cooking or salad greens with their leaves. The seeds of the black mustard, the more ancient one, are those used to make the mustard of commerce. Early gardeners ground their own mustard seed in what were called mustard mills, small grinders for which mortar and pestle may be substituted.

Old catalogs carried mustard, although it was listed as a minor garden item. An annual, mustard is easily available today, a sprightly-tasting and nutritious leafy green, but most frequently as a different and leafier species than the old white and black mustards. The mustard so often seen growing as a weed, bearing simple little yellow flowers, is apt to be the white or black mustard, and is a grateful dish, as old herbalists used to say of appetizing plants. Mustard of all kinds is quick to go to seed, especially in warm weather, so successive plantings are necessary for a continuing supply, and mid-summer plantings are of little avail. Grow mustard as you do lettuce.

NASTURTIUM

This amiable annual flower that gets along on the worst sort of soil if necessary was an inhabitant of many an early American household garden by the later 1700s if not considerably before then. The reason for the nasturtium's popularity was its dual use —flowers for bouquets, and flowers, leaves, and seeds for eating. The flowers and leaves went into salads, and the seeds were pickled after being picked green; so treated, they became a nice substitute for capers. Early seed catalogs called nasturtiums Indian cress also, and advised pickling the seeds in vinegar. To do so, cover a jar of them with boiling vinegar and store at room temperature. They will be ready in two weeks, and will keep for months.

A peculiar belief, alive in the 1830s, was that the brilliantly colored nasturtium flowers emitted flashes of light in the morning before sunrise and again at twilight.

New Zealand spinach has been in American gardens for about 150 years, a minor cooking green.

New Zealand Spinach

This annual vegetable (which comes back year after year like a perennial when grown in mild climates, we have found) appeared in American gardens early in the 19th century. It was found in New Zealand in 1770, but also grows in China, Japan, Australia, and Chile. Botanically *Tetragonia expansa*, it is called spinach only because, like spinach, it is a cooking green; unlike spinach, it will take hot weather but not cold.

The plant is a sprawling one unless it finds a fence to climb. The part eaten is the young growth, about the last 4″ of the leafy stems. Leaves are small, somewhat fleshy, and glisten with dots of moisture. Soak seed in warm water before planting in hills, like squash. Use plenty of compost, and half a dozen plants will supply the family. Most seed houses today carry New Zealand spinach—look under "spinach."

OKRA

By the middle of the 18th century, okra was in American gardens, specifically in Philadelphia. But the plant has always been more cultivated in the South than elsewhere, partly because warm southern summers suit it and partly because it became, early on, an important ingredient in some southern dishes such as gumbo. That lover of good food, Thomas Jefferson, knew okra from its being grown in Virginia before the end of the Revolutionary War. The plant is not one of ancient record, but may have been known for much longer than we can trace, and was almost certainly being grown by the Egyptians in the 13th century; tropical Africa is okra's place of origin.

The plant is a surprisingly good producer providing you keep the pods picked before they grow too large. It is an annual and does well in average garden soil. Seed it after the weather is warm in late spring; space plants 8″ apart and mulch with compost later on.

ONIONS

Onions were planted in the earliest gardens of New England, and seem to have been a universal colonial garden vegetable. This is what you'd expect, as the globe onion is a valued and old vegetable, reaching back into antiquity.

In addition, Welsh onions were also grown in American gardens by at least the 18th century. This is an onion whose hollow leaves are used much as chives are. Le Jardin is the only house we know of that lists this onion today.

Seed onions in compost-enriched soil and work a pound of cottonseed meal into each 20′ of row two months later. Bone meal and wood ashes were highly recommended as fertilizers years ago. This 19th-century advice about globe onions is still excellent: "Keep clean of weeds, and take care that the earth does not accumulate about the bulbs, but allow them to bottom above the ground." To do this, gently loosen the soil around the plants after bulbs have begun to form, so that bulbs can expand freely.

87

AMERICAN GROWN — PRIZETAKER ONION.

COPYRIGHTED BY 1891 W. ATLEE BURPEE & CO.

THE PRIZE=TAKER ONION.

The AMERICAN-GROWN PRIZE-TAKER ONION grows uniform in shape, of a nearly perfect globe, as shown in the illustration, with thin skin of bright straw color ; it is of immense size, measuring from twelve to eighteen inches in circumference, while under special cultivation specimen bulbs have been raised to weigh from four to five and a half pounds each. It ripens up hard and fine, and presents the handsomest possible appearance ; the flesh is pure white, fine grained, mild and delicate in flavor.

Per pkt. 10 cts.; per oz. 20 cts.; 2 ozs. 30 cts.; per ¼ lb. 50 cts.; per lb. $1.75, postpaid. By express, not prepaid, per lb. $1.65 ; 5 lbs. or more at $1.50 per lb.

THE PRIZE=TAKERS OF 1895.

In order to have thorough comparative tests of the PRIZE-TAKER and new GIBRALTAR ONIONS we offered last year a series of 21 prizes amounting to $260.00 for the best specimens of each variety. The competition, as will be seen from the awards, was widely conducted and the PRIZE-TAKER retained first place for size, the largest specimen weighing 5½ pounds, exactly one pound more than the heaviest *Gibraltar*. (See page 28.)

The *First Prize* of $35.00 was awarded to MR. W. J. PARKER, Woodland, N. C., for a fine globular onion weighing **5½ POUNDS, or 88 ounces.** The *Second Prize* of $20.00 to W. A. SHARPNACK, Alma, Neb., weight **50 ounces.** *Third Prize* of $15.00 to MR. ABEL STEELE, Ferguson, Ontario, Canada, weight **44 ounces.** *Fourth Prize* of $10.00 to MRS. JESSIE W. THORNTON, Oak Creek, Oregon, weight **40½ ounces.** Fifth, Sixth, Seventh, Eighth, Ninth, and Tenth Prizes, respectively, of $5.00 each, to JOSEPH BECK, New Bridge, Oregon, weight 40 ounces ; MRS. L. A. LEWIS, Cozad, Neb., weight 32 ounces ; ROBT. STIBBARD, Eglinton, Ontario, Canada, weight 32 ounces ; GEO. B. HUSTON, Arroyo Grande, Cal., weight 29 ounces ; MRS. A. J. HATHAWAY, Montalvo, Cal., weight 28 ounces, and MR. G. M. CHAFFIN, Phillipston, Mass., weight 26 ounces. The prize specimens, exhibited at our office side by side with the *New Gigantic Gibraltar Onions*, called forth the highest commendation.

Another onion authority of this same period confidently advised gardeners not to bother with thinning onions, for: "If the land is rich enough, the onions will grow and bottom in clusters and push each other sidewise; one onion will ride on top of two others, with its roots running down between them to the soil underneath." This is roughly our experience also, but we usually thin an onion bed anyway because the thinnings are nice green onions, handy to have in cooking. Cobbett also advised against thinning and said that by this system the onions "will not be large but they will be ripe earlier and will not run to neck."

ORACH

This ancient plant, now apt to be found listed among herbs—if found at all—used to be a familiar vegetable in the Old Country and was so used by early American gardeners. It was also called butter leaves, sea purslane, and French or mountain spinach. Its botanical name is *Atriplex hortensis*, and the young leaves were cooked like spinach.

Orach is an attractive and non-fussy plant, an annual that is seeded in spring and later thinned to 6" apart. The seeds are listed by le Jardin and Nichols.

PARSNIPS

Early American gardeners appreciated parsnips more than modern American gardeners do, and this old vegetable, grown as an annual, was among the first to be grown in American gardens. The parsnip had long been known as a wild plant, found in both Europe and North America.

Contrary to some modern advice, old seedsmen usually advised rich soil for parsnips. "It can hardly be made too rich," said

LEFT: *This onion, new in the 1890s, grew to such immense size that it was named "Prize-Taker," and some individual specimens weighed 4 or 5 pounds each.*

one. "Drop the seed in thickly," said another, "for where the seeds are few they are apt to perish in the ground, not having sufficient strength to open the pores of the earth." Parsnips should be seeded early, as they need the space all summer, but one of their merits is that they can be left in the garden all winter, to be dug as needed.

PEANUTS

This nutritious and appealing little foodstuff originated in South America and was a household garden plant in the early days of the United States and perhaps even before the Revolutionary War. Thomas Jefferson mentioned it as growing in Virginia at the close of the war. An annual, it does best where summers are long and warm. Nowadays Oklahoma claims to grow more peanuts than any other state.

In the second half of the 19th century, peanuts were sometimes found in the larger seed catalogs. Most houses carry them today, and northern gardeners can get a crop by planting in a sandy-soil spot (quick to warm in spring) close to a south wall for added warmth.

PEAS

Peas are another of the ancient annual vegetables, but enjoyed no great popularity in Europe until the 18th century. They seem to have been in American gardens in the 17th century, however, and some time during the 18th century, sugar peas, the edible-podded ones, were being grown here. Nineteenth-century seed catalogs carried many varieties of peas, including some still on the market, such as Telephone and Dwarf Gray Sugar.

Peas are a cool-weather crop, usually sown in the early spring. To spread the harvest, plant early peas, mid-season peas, and late peas all at the same time. Like beans, peas grown in fertile soil need only the fertilizing bestowed by dug-in compost when seeding. An old and good way with peas was to plant them where celery had been raised the year before, as celery needs extra-rich soil, and the fertility remaining, plug dug-in manure or compost, would be about right for the peas.

Sweet and hot peppers were in early American gardens and are thought to be native American plants. This one, offered in old catalogs, was one of the tomato-shaped types of sweet pepper.

PEPPERS

Peppers were known to early American gardeners and are probably a native vegetable of the American tropics. But the pepper, both sweet and hot kinds, will also grow in temperate climates when treated as annuals, and were listed by the 19th-century seedsmen in sometimes considerable variety, as nine sweet and six hot kinds in the 1880s by one large house. Some sixty years earlier, the home gardener had a choice of only five kinds altogether. Generally speaking, peppers were more cultivated in the southern parts of early America, becoming more widely grown by the early 19th century until their popularity was securely established—which it has remained. The advice of an old seedsman is still good: "It is desirable to start pepper plants in a hot bed and transplant as soon as the ground is warm and all danger of frost is over." But there are some faster-maturing kinds that can be seeded directly in the garden except in a very short-summer climate. Stokes lists one called Earliest Red Sweet, ma-

91

turing in 55 days, and the midget Vinedale is only five days behind it. Grow peppers as you grow tomatoes, except that no staking is needed.

POTATOES

White potatoes were already in America, waiting for colonial gardeners to find and appreciate them, for the potato originated in Chile, it is believed, and was brought to North America in the 16th century. Cultivation traveled northward from Florida through Virginia slowly, however, and the potato was not a common garden crop in New England until the 19th century was well under way. In fact, improved varieties came to America from Europe, where this native annual American vegetable had become well liked. This reputation took a while to grow, for some of the earliest potatoes were apt to be watery and of poor quality; it is this variation, we suspect, that led some 18th-century critics to say, having tasted only indifferent kinds of potatoes, that they were good only for swine.

Improvements in potatoes have come about mainly by planting the seeds the plants occasionally mature, and then by selecting the most promising of the new varieties thus formed. In this respect the potato is like a fruit tree, the seeds producing a variety different from the parent plant. Ordinary propagation of potatoes is a vegetative process, not a sexual one, done by planting chunks of potatoes, each having at least one eye, which is a bud that will form a plant. We were pleased to run across, in the 1920 Farmer Seed Company catalog, a listing of potato seed-ball seeds, offered gardeners as "a very interesting employment" in growing new varieties. "The result is often extremely profitable," said the catalog. The price was 10 cents a packet.

Nineteenth-century catalogs often gave much space to potatoes, the 1884 Burpee one listing 32 varieties. They included the famous Burbank potato, known as Burbank's Seedling, which had gone on the market about 10 years before. It was described

92

as "White-skinned, few eyes, fine-grained flesh; dry and floury when cooked; very productive." A related variety, Russet Burbank, is a leading potato today.

Early spring is the best time to plant potatoes in your garden. "Select warm, dry soil, and make it rich," ran the old advice, so dig compost in generously beforehand and plant chunks, eyes up, 2" to 4" deep and 10" apart in rows 2' apart. It is usually best to cut the chunks two days ahead of planting so they can air-dry a little. Harvest the crop when the tops turn yellow, which takes about three months.

The Farmer's Dictionary, by Isaiah Thomas, 1790, offered this cultural suggestion: "New method of planting potatoes is this, after dung is spread and ploughed in, raise ridges with the cultivator; dibble in the sets along top of ridges, about as deep as ridges are above surface before ridges were made. Cover with straw or old refuse hay to a depth of about 12 inches. Nothing more has to be done, until they are taken up—they will be clean and the crop considerable."

What we call stealing a crop of young potatoes early was well known to gardeners a century or more ago, and here are the directions from an 1871 garden guide: "In April, potatoes may be tried by scraping away the earth near the collar. The largest tubers are generally near the surface, and may be removed without disturbing the plants, which should be left to perfect the smaller ones; water, if required, but liquid manure is not necessary." Our own system is to tuck compost around the plants after the operation, and water them.

POTATOES, SWEET
(SEE SWEET POTATOES)

PUMPKINS
(SEE SQUASHES)

RADISHES

Even though it may seem a rather non-essential food, the radish was one of the annual vegetables the first American gardeners raised. The plant itself is ancient, very highly prized by the Greeks of antiquity and long before that by the Egyptians. In America toward the end of the 18th century, ten varieties of radishes were being grown, and probably many more. We counted 26 listed in an 1884 catalog. These included several winter radishes and a variety grown for the seed pods, the rat-tailed radish.

Radishes like soil rich in organic matter, plenty of moisture, and cool weather.

Not many gardeners today grow winter radishes, we find, but seeds continue to be offered by most seedsmen. These radishes grow large and can be stored in moist sand in the basement for winter. They need about two months to mature, twice as long as most early radishes, some of which are ready in under three weeks. Certain varieties of radishes grow quite large, and one you can find in some catalogs today is the Sakurajima, which is said to have reached 100 pounds, though 15 or 20 is more likely. Houses listing it include Burgess, de Giorgi, Field, Gurney, Nichols, and Shumway.

In 1880 a new radish was introduced by Burpee, called the Golden Globe, a nicely rounded radish with yellow skin but without any claim to great size. A Missouri customer, however, had no patience with such modesty, writing, "Some of my Golden Globe radishes measured 16 inches in circumference," or about the size of a grapefruit. An Arkansas customer reported growing ordinary spring radishes as "large as a quart bowl."

RASPBERRIES

An old fruit, in fact an ancient one, raspberries were in American gardens early on. The first species grown was the European, the American one coming later, both of them derived from wild types. Although it dislikes extremes of heat and cold, the raspberry is not fussy as to soil type. Spring planting is best, and the life of a planting is about 10 years. Space plants 5′ apart. There are red raspberries, black ones, purple ones, and yellow ones; each comes in both ever-bearing and one-crop types.

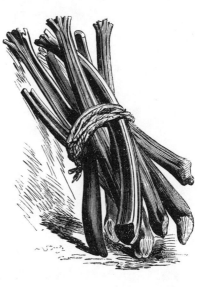

Rhubarb was one of the first vegetables ready in spring, so was especially important in early American gardens.

RHUBARB

Rhubarb, or pie plant, probably appeared in American gardens during the 18th century. It had been grown in England earlier, about the middle of the previous century, but as an ornamental. Rhubarb is an Asiatic plant, and was known in China and Russia in earlier times.

Most of the first American propagation was by seed—and indeed, rhubarb is still grown from seed by gardeners. But as with asparagus, the faster way is to plant 1-year-old roots, and this also ensures getting a rhubarb true to type, for the plant grown from seed is subject to variation.

Rhubarb is a perennial, occupying the same garden spot for six or eight years. After that it is best to move it elsewhere after cutting the roots into several pieces, each with a bud. Space the pieces 4′ apart. Thus you have a self-perpetuating crop. Dig the earth well when planting rhubarb, and work in plenty of compost; it can use a 4″ dressing of compost each fall and a lighter one in the spring as a mulch. After the first year of growth from a start with roots you can harvest rhubarb each spring until about June. Here is a 100-year-old tip on speeding your rhubarb harvest in spring: "A coldframe placed over rhubarb in April will bring it on fast."

Victoria is an old variety and is usually the one offered today as seed. Newer varieties are Canada Red, McDonald, and Valentine. Don't eat rhubarb leaves, by the way—just the stalks. The leaves contain oxalyic acid, which is toxic. They're all right for the compost pile, though.

ROCKET

This is one of the names by which an annual salad plant is known, also called rocket salad. Botanically *Eruca sativa*, it was in some of the earliest New England gardens and had been in English gardens for years before that, for it is an ancient vegetable. The plant wants cool weather but is otherwise undemanding. It was eaten both raw and as a cooked green. We have found no mention of it in old catalogs but it is listed today by de Giorgi as rocket salad, by Nichols as garden rocket, by Park as rocket or rucola, and Burpee and le Jardin list roquette, another name by which *Eruca sativa* is known. Grow it as you do spinach.

We have raised this vegetable and found it more a curiosity than useful. It is noted for its strong and distinctive smell. Fast growth and a cool season are said to reduce this.

RUTABAGA

By all accounts, rutabagas were not grown by early American colonists, although the plant was known in Europe early in the 17th century. An English gardener of the late 18th century tested on his dinner guests the new-to-him rutabagas he was growing in his garden, and said they preferred them to turnips and "thought the leaves equal to spinage." When the rutabaga did arrive in the United States, probably a little before the start of the 19th century, the white-rooted variety was known as turnip-rooted cabbage —the rutabaga being related to cabbage. This name was dropped in favor of simply "white rutabaga," spelled "ruta-baga" by 19th-century seedsmen. Today seed catalogs usually list only one or two yellow rutabagas, and white ones are scarce. Harris, however, carries Macomber, a very good white-fleshed one.

Sow rutabagas in mid-summer about three months before hard frost is expected. Care for them as you do turnips or beets, but they like a richer soil than the other two. Rutabagas are annuals, but if you protect them with a 6" mulch they can stay in the garden all winter, to be dug as wanted.

SALSIFY

This ancient annual root vegetable appears to have been among those in early American gardens, certainly toward the end of the 1700s. Oddly, for so good a food, salsify was not planted widely then nor is it now. (Another plant with a root tasting like salsify, called Spanish oyster plant, was also found in some early gardens, but not to any great extent. Black salsify, or scorzonera, was also in early gardens; it approximates salsify in flavor and is related to it. De Giorgi, Johnny, le Jardin, and Thompson & Morgan list it.)

Seed salsify in the spring, in soil well dug and enriched with compost and with one pound of cottonseed meal to 15' of row. Thin plants to 6" apart and give them a compost mulch when they are half grown. Salsify forms a beautiful ferny top, and will occupy the space all season. The roots, looking like parsnips, may be left in the garden all winter, lightly straw-mulched in cold climates; a freeze improves their flavor, which is oyster-like, and a cream soup made of them tastes much like an oyster stew. Boiled, mashed, and made into fritters, an old seedsman told his customers, "they are delicious."

Salsify or oyster plant is grown for its roots, used as are parsnips, or in a soup that tastes much like an oyster stew.

SEA-KALE

Until about 200 years ago, seakale (*Crambe maritima*) was known as a wild seacoast vegetable in Europe, but by late in the 18th century it was being grown in gardens and was in American gardens by at least 1806, as McMahon lists it. It was not in many gardens, however, then or now. Yet sea-kale has some good points to recommend it to gardeners: It is a perennial, needing no annual planting; its cropping season is in early spring, when garden-fresh vegetables are scarce; and it is good to eat.

The quickest way to get a crop is to plant root cuttings, but these are hard to find, and we know of only one source even for seed. Sow the seed in flats in March, indoors, or in peat blocks. Move the plants to the garden in about six weeks, spacing them

1½' to 2' apart in a spot where they won't be disturbed. Dig compost in generously beforehand, along with 1 cup of cottonseed meal in each spot. Give these young plants two years to grow and start cropping the third spring.

When the young shoots appear in early spring, blanch them by covering with earth or with boxes. This makes them tender. Snap them off near ground level when they are from a few inches to a foot tall, and cook them like asparagus. The harvesting can last till leaves begin to show up. Plants will then grow to an ultimate three feet high. Treat them like asparagus, letting them alone all summer, and cutting foliage to a few inches above ground level in late fall. A compost mulch at this time is welcome. Thompson & Morgan sell seeds of sea-kale.

Like leeks, shallots are patricians of the onion group, and were as much liked by good cooks of decades ago as by good ones today.

SHALLOTS

It is interesting to note that shallots were being grown by American gardeners enough for them to be included in McMahon's *American Gardener's Calendar* in 1806. We can safely presume that shallots were well known in American home gardens in the previous century, for they had been known in Europe from the time of the Crusades.

Also called eschalots, these highly prized little relatives of the globe onion recommended themselves to early and later American gardeners for their superb keeping qualities when well

99

dried. Shallots were also eaten in the green state, and it was in this way that early gardeners in the South used them, as do today's gardeners there and in other mild-weather regions.

Shallots are nearly always grown from bulbs and treated as annuals. They were not listed in most of the old catalogs we have seen, but trading among gardeners was a common way of obtaining starts. Plant and care for shallots like garlic, but give them less water. It still takes some searching to find shallot bulbs to plant (unless the produce department of your supermarket sells them), but here are five sources: Gurney (who also lists shallot seed), Hemlock Hill, le Jardin, Nichols, and Thompson & Morgan.

SKIRRET

This is a perennial vegetable, once grown for its roots, which look like small parsnips. The plant comes from China and was certainly in some early American gardens, but never widely grown. One reason for this is that skirret seeds sprout slowly and poorly, and the roots take more time to prepare for the table than, say, parsnips. An often used method was to cook the skirret roots tender in water, peel them, then dip in a batter and fry in butter. Cobbett said they were also put into soups.

·Today we know of only one source for skirret, Hemlock Hill, which offers plants. The plants need the summer to grow good roots, which can then be dug in the fall like horseradish. Also like horseradish, skirret forms small side roots that can be dug and planted in the spring to increase the bed.

SORREL

This perennial leafy green was in early American gardens, having been popular in Europe for centuries, but in time in America it came to be largely superseded by other plants. We came across it years ago, growing in the garden of some Dutch neighbors. Some 19th-century seed catalogs listed sorrel, but very few do today. Sorrel's flavor is bitter to some tastes, including ours, but the great popularity this vegetable has enjoyed suggests that it deserves a trial by any gardener interested in leafy greens; high in vitamin C, sorrel is also put into salads.

"Sow in spring," an old catalog instructed, "in drills eighteen inches apart, in a rich soil, and keep the flower stems cut off as they appear. It remains in the ground year after year, and only needs to be taken up and divided once in four or five years. Inasmuch as the hot sun tends to increase its acidity, a northern exposure is preferable." The plant grows to about 3' and is an attractive garden specimen. Give it a fairly dry spot. To increase the planting, divide roots in spring. De Giorgi and Nichols list it.

SPINACH

Spinach, cultivated in Europe since about the 13th century, was one of the annual plants in early American gardens, probably among the first to be planted. Old catalogs commonly listed spinach, although not in the great variety some other plants appeared.

Spinach likes cool weather, making it a spring plant or a fall one, and to grow good spinach, dig in plenty of compost before seeding. Late-seeded spinach will go through a surprising amount of cold weather if given a straw mulch. To get an early spring crop, even in cold-winter climates, follow this advice from an 1880s seedsman: "Early in the autumn select a sheltered location. Make the soil very rich—the richer the better. Drill in the seed in rows 15 inches apart. Sow plenty of seed and thin out the young plants from four to six inches apart in the rows. These young plants that you thin out are excellent for use. When winter sets in, cover the bed with some litter or straw. If the land is rich and the work properly done you will have a splendid crop."

SQUASHES AND PUMPKINS

There is no question that summer squashes, winter squashes, and pumpkins were some of the earliest garden vegetables in

Winter squashes have always come in a variety of sizes, shapes, and colors. This one, no longer on the market, was called the Olive, presumably for its shape and color.

America, but nobody is very sure where they originated. The Indians were well acquainted with these annual crops for centuries before Europeans arrived in the Americas, and some researchers conclude from this and other evidence that the plants are, like common beans and Jerusalem artichokes, native Americans.

Summer squashes seem mainly to have been the pattypan and yellow crookneck types in early days, and the word "squash" was applied to them, whereas "pumpkin" was used for winter squashes as well as for what we call pumpkins today.

Early seedsmen were apt to pay more attention to winter squashes than to summer ones, a very good reason for this being the superb keeping quality of the latter, needing nothing more than a frost-free place to stay good for months. The Hubbard, introduced in 1857, became the standard of excellence among winter squashes, and has continued to be popular ever since, although there are now some extremely good and more conveniently sized rivals such as Butternut and Buttercup.

Pumpkins, which also keep well, were accordingly very popular with early and later American gardeners. In his *Handbook of Plants*, Peter Henderson wrote of pumpkins in 1881: "Three hundred years ago they were made into pies by cutting a hole in the side, extracting the seeds and filaments, stuffing the cavity with apples and spices, and baking the whole." Some later specimens such as of the variety called Mammoth Tours, weighed over 300 pounds, an enormous lot of nutritious and tasty winter food for a family, though not in a single pie as above. "The competition among gardeners for large and good pumpkins for the Paris markets is quite interesting," observed Mr. Burpee in 1884 of French farmers, "the largest being crowned 'King of Pumpkins.' "

Today the pumpkin is a minor home garden crop, with small-sized varieties most popular, and summer squashes have passed winter ones in garden frequency.

Each of these crops takes the same general care as cantaloupes and cucumbers, but give winter squashes a heavy mulch of compost and ½ pound of cottonseed meal per hill when half grown. As with watermelons, old advice was to pinch off tips of shoots on vining types in order to promote fruiting and early maturing. Do this after the plants flower.

STRAWBERRIES

Although apparently known to the ancient Romans, the strawberry did not come into prominence in Europe until the Middle Ages, and then more as a wild plant than a cultivated one. The delectable little fruit was also growing wild in America and was eaten by the early colonists. Some Indian tribes in the Northeast also cultivated strawberries, but the development of a host of improved varieties did not take place until the 19th century was under way.

By the 1880s one nurseryman typical of others could assure

his customers: "With berries as large as small apples, with the spice and aroma of Ambrosia, we scarcely realize the wonders of the soil, and with what little labor it is developed. No one knows the enjoyment of Strawberries unless picked from your own vines. Even a dozen hills, well taken care of, will produce an enormous quantity of berries."

Except for Alpine strawberries, for which you can get seed, strawberries are commonly grown from plants that are formed from runners the mother plants grow during the summer. A planting will last about three seasons, and will grow its own replacement plants. June-bearing strawberries give a big crop in, usually, June. Everbearers space the crop from spring to fall.

Set strawberry plants in early spring 18″ apart, with the crowns (the "waist," between top and roots) halfway in the ground. Keep blossoms picked off the first season for a better crop the next year, and give each plant a tablespoon of blood meal in August. Repeat this feeding the next year after harvest.

SUNFLOWERS

Sunflower seeds have been eaten by their fanciers for years, but in early America the unopened flower buds formed an article of food. They probably were a minor such item, but this use had been known in England in the 16th century. The buds were either broiled or cooked in water. You grow sunflowers, which are annuals, as you do corn.

SWEET POTATOES

Originating in the American tropics, the sweet potato, like America, was discovered by Christopher Columbus. Because sweet potatoes need a long warm summer, this was a garden crop particularly favored by early American gardeners in the southern and middle colonies, and today the sweet potato is still thought of as a southern plant. However, it can be grown as far north as where there are five months of growing weather—so that plants given a headstart indoors have enough time to mature tubers before frost.

The plants do best with 175 frost-free days to make a crop, just about a garden record for leisurely production.

Sprouts grow from a last-year's sweet potato, and these are what you plant for this year's crop. It is also possible to grow a plant by half-burying a 15" piece of vine from another plant. You may be able to buy sprouts locally, but if not, they can be ordered from Burgess, Field, or Olds.

(See Chapter 6 for directions on harvesting and storing sweet potatoes.)

TANSY

This inhabitant of an occasional herb garden today was an esteemed minor vegetable in earlier days. It gradually declined in popularity as the 19th century wore on, until it became what it now is, a mere garden curiosity or a weedy escape. In fact it is looked on as poisonous by some. An old materia medica we checked stated it was dangerous in "large doses." The young leaves of tansy used to be employed in various dishes, especially in the springtime, and eggs often figured in the preparation, as with omelets and puddings.

Tansy is a perennial, about 3' tall with button-like yellow flowers and a decided foliage fragrance. It wants sun and will grow easily from seed, but we know of only plant sources— Hemlock Hill and Nichols.

TOMATOES

A native of tropical America, the tomato came to the attention of Europe in the 16th century, and a very curious attention it got. Hardly anyone considered these brightly colored fruits fit to eat; then as now, tomatoes came in colors of red, white, and yellow, and were called golden apples by some. The famed English herbalist Gerarde observed: "They yield very little nourishment to the bodie, and the same naught and corrupt."

Small wonder then that it took tomatoes until the 1830s to make much headway with American gardeners—even though

105

COPYRIGHTED 1888
W. ATLEE BURPEE & CO.

THE MATCHLESS TOMATO

THE MATCHLESS TOMATO.

As grown by us, from carefully selected Stock-Seed, THE MATCHLESS TOMATO is well worthy of its name; in beauty of coloring and symmetry of form it is indeed without a peer. The vines are of strong, vigorous growth, well set with fruit; the foliage is very rich dark green in color. The engraving accurately shows the shape and also the remarkable solidity of a section. They are entirely free from core, of a very rich cardinal-red color, and are not liable to crack from wet weather. The fruits are *of the largest size*, and *the size of the fruit is maintained throughout the season*, the healthy growth of foliage continuing until killed by frost. Had we to confine ourselves to one variety it would be THE MATCHLESS, for certainly *no other Tomato will produce extra large fruits, so smooth, handsome, and marketable, as The Matchless.* The skin is remarkably tough and solid, so that ripe specimens picked from the vine *will keep in good, marketable condition for two weeks.* Its fine quality and solidity are unequaled.

Per pkt. 10 cts.; 3 pkts. for 25 cts.; per oz. 35 cts.; 2 ozs 60 cts.; ¼ ℔ $1.00; per ℔ $3.50.

WHICH IS THE BEST?

The universal popularity of the Tomato naturally makes great rivalry among growers. ☞ The multiplication of varieties tends to confuse purchasers, and therefore in recommending THE MATCHLESS we would plainly state that we have tested it during the past six seasons at FORDHOOK FARM alongside of all known varieties, including such new sorts as *Aristocrat,—Crimson Cushion,—Liberty Bell,—Buckeye State,—Cumberland Red,—Early Michigan,—Great B. B.,—Shenandoah,—Early Emery,—Royal Red,—The Majestic,—Picture Rock,—Table Queen,—Belmont,—Henderson's Ruby,—Ten Ton,—The Money-Maker,—Prize-Taker,—World's Fair,—Red Cross,—Ruby Queen,—Early Champion,—South Jersey,—Brandywine,—Mitchell's New Tomato,—Logan Giant,—Two-pound,—Columbian Prize,—Bright and Early,—Landreth's Hybrids,* and *The Comrade,* with the result that our answer is, that (when grown from *pure, selected stock,* such as ours) the very best bright-red Tomato in cultivation to-day is THE MATCHLESS.

that indefatigable experimenter Thomas Jefferson recorded in 1781 that he was raising them in his garden. Here and there a few other daring souls were growing and praising the vegetable that is now the most popular of all among American home gardeners. Rather oddly, another early American name for the tomato was Jerusalem apple; like Jerusalem artichokes, this other native American vegetable had nothing at all to do with Jerusalem.

This tomato was a bush or tree type, offered about a century ago as Laye's Upright Red. Stakeless tomatoes are also on today's market, as plants that stay fairly small, usually under 2' tall.

The early American tomatoes were ribbed and flattened types, the round ones coming along later. Seed catalogs of the 1880s often carried a good selection of tomatoes, a dozen or more, but this was small indeed compared to onions and cabbages, which dominated page after page. Today every seed house is strong in tomatoes, and one, Stokes, lists nearly a hundred. Even by 1901 Mr. Burpee was able to state: "The tomato now rivals all other vegetables and fruits in popularity, having reached a use beyond that of the potato and apple combined."

Tomatoes are grown as annuals, and to start them from

LEFT: *Developed in the late 1880s, this fine red tomato was a big seller to American home gardeners for years.*

seed, plant the seed indoors six to ten weeks before the weather is due to turn mild. Then set the plants in the garden deeply, up to the lowest leaves, digging half a bucket of compost into each planting spot. Good old advice was that rich soil grew more tomatoes but delayed their ripening. Consequently, in fertile soil, compost alone will usually be enough fertilizer for the season. Set stakes for later support when you set out the plants. An alternative that was once used is this: "Drive two or three stakes around each plant, and encircle with as many barrel hoops."

Turnips have always been popular with American gardeners, the leaves being even more nutritious than the flavorful roots.

TURNIPS

Turnips were among the very first settlers in American gardens and have enjoyed an uninterrupted association with them ever since. Being a most obliging vegetable as to climate, the turnips settled happily in gardens from New England to Florida in the early times, and moved west with the pioneers, too.

An annual, the turnip is an old vegetable, and it or its ancient relatives had been feeding man and his beasts for many centuries in the Old World. Siberia seems to be where turnips came from in the first place. You grow turnips the way you grow beets.

Raising enormous specimens was something of a gardeners' sport long ago. Thirty-pounders were not unusual, and in 1850 one of a hundred pounds was reported grown in California. It is possible that these monsters were rutabagas, which are related to turnips and were called late turnips or Swede turnips by some old seedsmen. Like rutabagas, turnips can be kept in the garden over the winter by protecting them with a 6″ mulch.

Seedsmen of the last century were sometimes very big on turnips, and we counted 25 varieties listed in one old catalog. Among them was Cowhorn, "Of rapid growth, flesh white, sweet, delicate and rich flavor . . . roots shaped like a carrot and grow half above the ground," and Golden Ball or Orange Jelly, "Rich, sweet, pulpy flesh; of quick growth and keeps well." Both these varieties are listed today by Shumway. Olds also lists Cowhorn, and Nichols lists Golden Ball.

VINE PEACH

This annual vegetable is a relative of the cantaloupe and has also been variously known as mango melon, vegetable peach, vegetable orange, and by other names. Botanically it is *Cucumis chito*. The fruit looks a good deal like a peach but has a hard shell and is grown largely for making preserves and pies. It has never been widely grown, but was known to 19th-century and early-20th-century gardeners. Here is an excellent description from Vaughan's 1894 catalog:

"This peculiar new vegetable grows on a vine like a melon, and is of golden yellow color, resembling an orange in shape and size; the flesh is snow white. They are used fried like the egg plant when green. They also make splendid mangoes stuffed with cabbage like peppers. When they first ripen they are quite hard and tasteless, but they soon become mellow and sweet and have a very rich flavor. For sweet pickles, pies, or preserving, they have no equals. They are very early, hardy, and productive, the vines being literally covered with fruit."

You grow this vegetable as you do cantaloupes. Seeds are available from Burgess and Shumway.

WATER CRESS

Although it seems doubtful that water cress was in many of the earliest American gardens, this ancient perennial plant was being cultivated here to some extent in the 18th century. It grows naturally in running water and will become wild in a favorable situation—if not already present, for it is native to the northern temperate climates.

Seed of water cress was listed by the old seed catalogs and is listed by many houses today. Plants can be started from the seeds by sowing in sand that is kept constantly moist, as in a clay pot of sand set in a pan of water. Such plants can then be moved to a stream bank where the water will flow over the planting site—or this can be done with stems of mature water cress, which will often root when planted. It is so frequently said that water cress can also be grown in a merely damp location or around the edge of a pool, that we suppose it must be done, but it has never worked for us. We have had good results only in a spring (the water being about 60° F.), and in the creek the spring formed.

WATERMELONS

Popular in the Old World for centuries, the watermelon, a native of tropical Africa, came across the Atlantic with early colonists and was one of the common annual garden fruits in early-17th-century New England. In Egypt, indeed, this fruit that we now think of as a summertime pleasure was the principal food and drink of the populace for several of the warm months.

Plant and care for watermelons as you do cantaloupes. Watermelons prefer a more acid soil, and a simple old way to get it is to dig a half bucket of sawdust into the spot when planting seed. Old instructions read: "Set the seeds edgewise with the eyes down." To promote growth of the fruits and earlier maturity, another old suggestion was: "After the flowers appear, pinch off the extreme end of the most luxuriant shoots."

The early American watermelons were not immense by later standards, when 100 pounds became attainable, but there seems to have been some variation of flesh color, ranging from white through peach to red. Yellow-fleshed watermelons were also known 200 years ago, although still regarded as novel today, along with white-fleshed ones. Also it is interesting to note that modern tastes and space have brought the small watermelon to the front again. You can still get seed to grow a big one such as Black Diamond that can go to 125 pounds (Park carries it), but among the popular varieties today are the 5-pound New Hampshire Midget, carried by most houses, and the 12-pound Northern Sweet (Burgess, Gurney, and Olds).

From the number of watermelon varieties offered the old-time gardener—35 in one catalog alone—it seems as if no home was a home without a vine. Varieties included Hungarian Honey, Vick's Early, and The Boss among small melons, and some large to huge sizes were Duke Jones, Sweet Heart, and Ice Cream. Then, as today, gardeners needed all the help they could get on judging watermelon ripeness, and the catalogs were free with advice: The melon was ripe when the tendril at the stem end turned brown; when the part resting on the earth turned from white to yellow; when a knuckle rap produced a hollow "thunk"; and when pressing down on the melon produced a cracking sound. Plugging was also mentioned, but as a rather unsporting alternative.

Good Old Kitchen
Herbs for Today

THE herbs discussed here are
those used principally for flavoring dishes—one of the important
roles of herbs in early American households. Because some other
plants that are now classed as flavoring herbs were years ago
being grown as cooking or salad greens, we put them among the
food plants in Chapter 4. And the herbs used for still other purposes—cosmetics, medicines, and so on—will be found in
Chapter 7.

ANISE

An inhabitant of early American
gardens, anise had a minor but
popular use as a flavoring. The leaves were put in salads and the
seeds flavored cakes and breads. Anise is an annual, seeded when
weather is mild. It is another of the ancient herbs, and its name is
sometimes, mistakenly, applied to fennel. (See Chapter 7 for
anise's use as a tea.)

BALM

Also called lemon balm, this perennial herb has a nice lemony taste. It was in American gardens by the 18th century and almost certainly earlier, for balm is an ancient plant and famous for attracting bees. As a herb it was used much as lemon thyme was used, an agreeable seasoning for delicately flavored vegetables and in salads. (See Chapter 7 for balm's use as a tea, a medicine, and in vinegar.)

Balm is grown by seeding or by root division, and has a name for running rampant in rich soil. Seed is carried by Burgess, Johnny, le Jardin, Nichols, Olds, and Park; plants are offered by Hemlock Hill and Nichols.

BASIL

By the 18th century, basil was well known in American gardens. It was used in salads and with cooked vegetables, including tomatoes after they came into good standing with housewives in the 19th century. (See Chapter 7 for the use of basil in vinegar.) Basil is available in several varieties including a dwarf, a lettuce-leaved, and a purple-leaved kind, and is a delightful plant to smell in the garden. An annual, it grows readily from seed but demands warm weather. Don't seed it until the soil warms in the spring.

BEE BALM

This perenial herb is listed in Chapter 7, for a tea.

BORAGE

Borage is a plant the ancients prized, using its leaves and pretty blue flowers in wines—as borage was called a temperate herb, and Pliny said it made the drinker joyful. In Queen Elizabeth I's England the leaves went into salads, and they still do today, having a mild cucumber flavor. The early American gardeners raised borage, an annual that is a willing grower and a pretty garden plant except that it may grow too lustily for the space you can spare it, and is a vigorous self-seeder. One old use of borage was to make candy of the flowers (described in Chapter 7).

BURNET

Now classed as a herb, burnet, a perennial, was once used to flavor ale, the leaves being the part employed. Since they were also used in salads, we cover burnet in Chapter 4.

CALENDULA

This annual flower, also called pot marigold, was grown for culinary purposes by American gardeners in earlier times. The richly yellow petals colored butter, were a substitute for saffron, and were included in cooked dishes for their savory flavor. Cobbett wrote in 1821 that the petals should be pulled off the flowers when they are in full bloom, dried in the shade, and stored in paper bags. "They are excellent in broths, and soups, and stews," he said. (See Chapter 7 for medical use.) The calendula is easily grown from seed planted in late spring in ordinary garden soil.

CAMOMILE

See Chapter 7 for camomile flower tea, and for the herb, a perennial, as an insect repellent.

CARAWAY

The seeds of caraway, a biennial, were used for seasoning rye bread, and years ago the leaves for flavoring some alcoholic drinks. (See Chapter 4 for other uses of caraway.)

CHERVIL

This attractive little annual herb's leaves are used to flavor a variety of meat and vegetable dishes, and are sometimes chopped into salads. (See Chapter 7 for medical use.)

CHIVES

Chives were grown in colonial American gardens and had been in European gardens for centuries. Although probably not of great garden interest where every inch of space counted, the plant is a non-demanding perennial that would grow in an idle corner of the dooryard, so could justify itself as to room. Old catalogs offered seeds, as do catalogs today. A quicker start is had by getting plants, easily found at local garden supply shops. Plants grow into clumps that should be divided and transplanted every second or third spring.

CLARY

This biennial herb's leaves flavored drinks, omelets, and fritters, tasting something like sage, to which clary is related. (See Chapter 4 for culture and other uses, and Chapter 7 for clary tea and in potpourris.)

COMFREY

Thought of as a perennial herb today, comfrey was once used as a cooking green, and so is listed in Chapter 4. (See also Chapter 7 for medical uses.)

CORIANDER

This annual herb was being grown in Britain in ancient days, perhaps introduced there by the Romans, who flavored food with coriander seeds. The plant was grown in early American gardens, in the 17th century, the young leaves going into salads and soups, and the ripe seeds imparted a somewhat orange-like flavor to candies.

COSTMARY

Not much seen today, this perennial herb was in at least some American gardens in the mid-19th century. The leaves were sometimes put into salads, and flavored ale and beer, alecost being another name for the plant. It is also called Bible leaf, and

115

mint geranium. (See Chapter 7 for cosmetic use, and as a fragrance.) Multiplication is by root division. We know of two sources for plants, Hemlock Hill and Nichols.

DILL

Dill is an old herb and was probably in the earliest American gardens. Its leaves were used in some soups and in sauces for fish, and the ripe seeds flavored dill pickles. Dill is an annual that grows easily from seed sown in spring; we have found it avid to come back each year from seed it drops.

FENNEL

The herb is the sweet fennel, a relative of Florence fennel. Sweet fennel is a perennial. The part used for flavoring dishes is the foliage, which enters into some fish sauces. Fennel seeds are sometimes used to flavor liqueurs. Fennel is recorded as being in American gardens of the later 18th century and was probably in much earlier ones, as it had been well known to 11th-century Anglo-Saxons. Testifying to the popularity of the herb in the 1830s and earlier, a gardener wrote *Park's Floral Magazine:* "In old times every one had a patch of fennel, dill, or smellage [celery] to take to church, and when the wee ones got restless, a head of fennel or a sprig of dill was given them by mother or grandmother to keep them still."

FENUGREEK

This little-known plant, from Europe and the Orient, arrived in a few American gardens at about the time of the Civil War. In India the leaves were cooked like spinach, but it was the seeds the plant was grown for in most areas, for flavoring food. When ground, they are said to give a maple syrup flavor. We are skeptical of this use, as fenugreek is an old medicinal plant that figures in some ointments. Also, "The seed is often used to give temporary fire and vigor to horses," and old seedsman advised, and fed to cattle being fattened, as it made them drink more water.

116

But another use of fenugreek, for humans, is the production of sprouts from the seeds. Sprouts are rich in vitamins and protein. They can be cooked, or added to salads.

Fenugreek has never been seen much in gardens in this country, but seeds are still available, from Johnny, Nichols, and Thompson & Morgan. The plant is an annual, looks like sweet clover, and is seeded in April.

HOREHOUND

A perennial herb, horehound is listed in Chapter 7 for its medical values.

HYSSOP

This perennial herb, now seldom seen, was once fairly frequent in American gardens and was well known in the Old World since ancient times, if there is no confusion of terms. The herb was valued for medicinal use (see Chapter 7) and appears in early 20th-century materia medicas, but it was also used in the kitchen in early America. The aromatic young leaves were put into soups, stews, and salads. Hyssop is attractive in the garden, growing to about 2' high and having spikes of small white, blue, purple, or pink flowers according to the variety, all summer. It is much admired by bees. De Giorgi, Johnny, le Jardin, and Park list hyssop seed, Hemlock Hill carries plants, and Nichols carries both.

LAVENDER

Though not used to flavor foods, lavender is listed in Chapter 7 as a source of fragrance and medicine. it is a perennial.

LOVAGE

Young stems and seeds of lovage were used to flavor foods years ago, the seeds in cakes, candy, and sometimes meat dishes. The herb was used more as celery is, however, and is listed in Chapter 4 as a perennial food plant.

Marjoram, a half-hardy perennial herb, has long been one of the more popular seasoning plants of the American home garden.

MARJORAM

Also called sweet marjoram, this aromatic little herb, a half-hardy perennial, was well known to 18th-century American gardeners. It dries well, and was used both dry and fresh for flavoring soups and salads, and in stuffings for fowl. (Also see Chapter 7 for medical uses and in vinegar.) Marjoram grows readily from seed sown directly in the garden in late spring, and in a mild climate it winters over and forms nice thrifty clumps that can be divided to multiply the planting.

A quality of marjoram as a fisherman's friend that we had never heard of was given by Anne Pratt in 1847 in *The Field, the Garden, and the Woodland:* "There are some kinds of fish that are so fascinated by the scent of sweet marjoram that, upon plunging into the water the hand that has been rubbed with it, the fish will come in numbers and suffer themselves to be taken."

MINTS

Of the various mints, catnip, peppermint, and spearmint appear to have been the ones in American gardens by at least the 18th century but probably considerably sooner, especially spearmint, the one most used at the table. All are perennials. Mint leaves were put in some sauces, and went toward flavoring peas and some root vegetables. Leaves were also dried for the same uses in winter. The plants can be grown from seed, root or stem cuttings, or by divisions of plants. (See Chapter 7 for mint in tea, in vinegar, medically, and as a fly chaser, and catnip as a tobacco substitute and medicine.)

ORACH

This annual herb is listed in Chapter 4 as a food plant.

A plant of plain-leaf parsley, also called Italian parsley.

PARSLEY

This is another of the herbs loved by the ancients, who used it extensively in salads and sauces, and believed it prevented drunkeness. Since parsley reached England in the mid-16th century, it is possible it was in early American gardens, though we have found no sure record of its being there before some time in the later 18th century. At that time both the curled-leaf and plain-leaf parsleys were being grown here, as was the parsley grown for its root, called Hamburg or turnip-rooted parsley.

Parsley is a biennial, going to seed the second year, so seed some each spring for use later that season and the first part of the following season. The seed takes up to three weeks to sprout, and

119

to make sure it doesn't dry out, we seed it in a flat, cover it with sheet plastic, and move plants to the garden later.

Useful as a seasoning and also in medicinal ways, rosemary has been in American gardens for many years and was well known in the pre-18th century Old World.

ROSEMARY

This half-hardy perennial herb, well known to the ancients, was in early American gardens and had a name for years as a welcome seasoning for meats. We have found it an agreeable herb in our own cooking, especially with chicken and lamb. In addition, rosemary had other uses (covered in Chapter 7), for which it would have recommended itself to colonists as well as to American gardeners who followed them. The history of rosemary is packed with virtues ascribed to it, such as an ability to improve the memory and as an emblem of wisdom and affection. Although we do not know if the custom was brought to young America, in England at about the 17th century, rosemary was carried by wedding guests.

RUE

See Chapter 7 for use of rue, a perennial, as an insect repellent.

120

SAGE

Sage was one of the herbs most highly thought of by ancient civilizations and was among the plants in early American household gardens, being an almost invariable ingredient of stuffings for fowl. The leaves are the part so used, fresh or dried, and they were also put into sausages and some cheeses. (See Chapter 7 for sage in tea, as a fly repellent, a medicine, and a tobacco substitute.) The plant is a hardy perennial, and we have found it willing to flourish even in poor clay soil. It can be started from seed, and the bed increased by rooting cuttings.

Summer savory is a nice annual herb, famous for how well it goes with green beans.

SAVORY

This agreeable herb was in early American gardens, both in the form of summer savory, an annual, and winter savory, a perennial. Summer savory is perhaps more delicate as a flavoring, and is much more often seen today. The leaves have long been used with green beans, and we find them good with many other vegetable dishes. (See Chapter 7 for medical uses.) Both kinds of savory can be started from seed sown directly in the garden when spring weather is mild.

121

SESAME

See Chapter 7 for use of this annual herb as a cosmetic and medicine.

TANSY

This perennial herb is listed among edibles in Chapter 4, and in Chapter 7 as a repellent of flies, and a medicine.

The elegant herb tarragon is a little hard to grow in some spots, but well worth the trouble.

TARRAGON

The tarragon most used in cooking, *Artemisia dracunculus*, arrived in England in the mid-16th century, and was in colonial American gardens by at least the 18th century. This plant is a perennial multiplied not by seeds but by dividing the root mass. Popular for flavoring vinegar, tarragon leaves are also used in salads, fish dishes, and omelets. (See Chapter 7 for use in vinegar.)

Cobbett said of tarragon: "It is eaten with beefsteaks in company with minced shallots. A man may live very well without it, but an Englishman once told me that he and six others once [ate] some beefsteaks with shallots and tarragon and they voted unanimously that 'beefsteaks never were so eaten!' "

We find tarragon a temperamental grower that has done best for us in sunny spots where it can get its roots against a concrete foundation wall, although some gardeners find it prefers part shade. Tarragon plants are listed by Burpee, Hemlock Hill, and le Jardin.

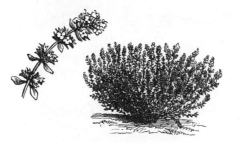

One of the best known herbs, thyme was in American gardens from earliest days and had many uses in the home.

THYME

Various kinds of thyme were in the first household gardens of America, the herb being one of those long cultivated in Europe. Thyme has many uses in the kitchen and was popular as a seasoning for fish and in sauces. We use it in these ways and in stews, and with many vegetables. (See Chapter 7 for thyme in tea, as a medicine, and in vinegar.) Except in the coldest winter climates thyme is a perennial. It can be raised from seed, and plants can be divided each year. Common thyme (*Thymus vulgaris*) and the closely related lemon thyme are the two we have found most useful in the kitchen.

CHAPTER
SIX

Tried and True Ways
of Winter Storage

IN 1920, two years after the
end of the First World War, even with postwar prices straining
family pocketbooks, the Farmer Seed Company could state in its
catalog: "An ordinary family of five would require during the
winter vegetables which would cost them from $20 to $40 if they
were to buy these at retail." Today the figures could be $100 to
$200. And, still as true as it was even 200 years ago, the convenience
and satisfaction of a well-stocked winter larder from your
own garden, is very special and a peculiar comfort that answers
old human urges.

In harvesting for storage, the first rules are: store only the
best, and handle with care. During a long winter's storage, any
little bruise can and usually will strike inward and bring loss
through spoilage. (There will be some shrinkage, but this is normal.)

Storage conditions depend on the crop, and may be moist,
dry, warm, or cool, in various combinations. The old outdoor pit
storage supplied the moist-and-cool combination, as did an earth-

floored cellar. A spare room was cool and dry. So were some basements. Spots near the kitchen range, and later near the cellar furnace, were warm and dry. We give the best storage conditions for each crop in the list that follows.

For some crops, storage right in the garden where they are growing is best. Parsnips are among these, and so are kale, spinach, Jerusalem artichokes, horseradish, and others mentioned below.

A few crops can be stored, in a sense, by sprouting their roots during the winter. Among them are asparagus, rhubarb, and witloof chicory, and we give directions.

In the 1890s commercial seed growers dried, or "cured," their seeds in the open air, as shown here, spreading them on tarpaulins laid on the ground and in shallow raised trays. The method is still used by some home gardeners who save their own seed.

Some crops must be dried to be stored, such as some beans and most herbs. Others, as detailed below, can be dried as an alternative to other kinds of storage methods. Whenever oven drying is mentioned hereafter, and two temperatures are given, the drying is to be started and finished at the *lower* temperature; the

125

middle two-thirds of the time, the higher temperature is the setting. Thus, for a 12-hour drying at 130°-150° F., dry for 2
hours at 130° F., then for 8 hours at 150° F., and finally for 2
more hours at 130° F.

Pickling was another favorite way of preserving, and the old
catalogs kept this in mind. Speaking of cucumbers for pickling,
one said: "In gathering, cut the stem instead of pulling the fruit
off and be careful not to mar the fruit in any way, for if the skin
be broken the pickles will not keep so well." To pickle a vegetable, it was soaked in brine for a day or more, sometimes cooked,
then put into crocks or jars and covered with hot vinegar to which
was usually added flavorings, among which were sugar, horseradish, hot peppers, spices. For fruits the brining was omitted
and the sugar was increased, to make a syrup with the vinegar.

ASPARAGUS

Fresh asparagus can be produced
in the cellar during winter by
digging roots in the fall, moving them to boxes of soil in the
cellar, putting them in a warm place near a window, and keeping
the earth moist. This process exhausts the root, so it is a good
idea to grow some roots just for this purpose rather than to dig
them from an established bed. You can grow roots most cheaply
by planting seed.

BEANS

The beans intended to be dried
for future use are listed as shell
beans in seed catalogs. These include pinto beans, kidney beans,
and navy beans. You can also dry lima beans. Three months or
longer is a usual maturity time for shell beans. When pods are
dry to the touch but less than bone-dry, cut them from the plant
with pruning shears and heap them in a carton to finish drying.
When they feel brittle, shell them, spread them in a baking pan,
and give them an hour in a 140° F. oven. Store them in jars or
cans at room temperature.

Green snap beans can be dried by stringing the whole pods on threads and hanging them in an airy place. For oven drying, cut pods in 1″ lengths after removing tip ends, and give them 3 to 5 hours at 130°-150° F.

BEETS

A 6″ straw mulch over the beet bed will protect it enough in all but the coldest winter climates. Or for kitchen convenience, dig the beets, clip off all but 1″ of the tops, and store the roots in the cellar in moist sand.

BRUSSELS SPROUTS

This plant is left in the garden, being tolerant to cold to about 10° F. above zero.

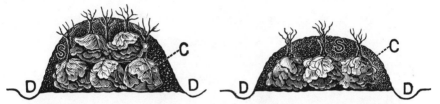

Outdoor winter storage of cabbage. One or two layers of upside-down heads are covered with earth, and drainage ditches are dug alongside at ground level.

CABBAGE

"Cabbage keeps best in moist, cool storage," an old seedsman said. "Pull them up by the roots in dry weather; they can then be hung in the cellar; or placed there, roots down, in a box of moist sand; or stored in a trench in the garden roots up and well covered with a thick straw mulch topped with some waterproof top such as tarpaper."

CARDOON

Dig up a few plants in the fall and grow them in a box of earth in the cellar, where they will self-blanch if the light isn't strong.

127

CARROTS

Store carrots as you do beets.

CAULIFLOWER

"Should some of the plants fail to head before the ground freezes," ran old directions, "take them up with a large ball of earth attached to the roots and put them into a coldframe or cellar, where small, tender heads will form during winter." Mature cauliflowers can be stored like cabbages, but for only about a month.

CELERIAC

"To keep through the winter, cover with earth and straw, like beets, or store in the cellar in damp sand," was the word from a 19th-century seedsman, as to celeriac.

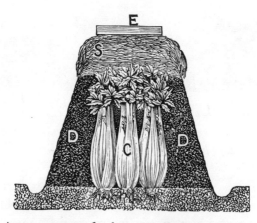

Outdoor winter storage of celery. Walled with earth, the celery is then given a straw roof topped with a board.

CELERY

This method of keeping fresh celery in the garden in the Rochester, New York, climate during the winter was given by the seedsman Joseph Harris in 1880: "Dig a narrow trench on dry land. Then put in the celery, standing up as it grew, side by side. Press the roots firm together, and cover the trench with boards. We usually put on the top bundles of cornstalks, and cover the whole with leaves, straw, or any other material that will keep out frost." Another version of this method is to set the celery inside a coldframe, deeply enough so the plant tops are about 4" below the sash. We have also kept celery for several weeks by planting the bunches side by side in a box of moist sand in the basement. If you do not have too severe a winter, a 2' straw mulch on a celery bed may be all the protection it needs.

CHICORY

As described in Chapter 4, roots of witloof chicory are sprouted for winter use by planting them in a keg of earth in the cellar and covering them with 8" of sawdust, which is kept moist. Sand can be used to cover them, and so can earth. An old seedsman offered this alternative in 1896, referring to roots allowed to remain in the garden where they had grown during the summer—as can be done in mild climates: "If quicker growth is desired, cover surface of soil with manure to a depth of sixteen inches to three feet, and in a month's time remove this covering, when the blanched heads will be found ready for use." This method could be followed in a trench dug in the garden also, or in colder climates, in a coldframe.

COLLARDS

Collards are left in the garden, as they are blessedly unhurt by frost and can take cold to 10° F. above zero. For colder weather give them a straw mulch.

CORN

To dry corn, blanch it on the cob for 5 minutes in boiling water, then cut the kernels off with a sharp knife and give them 4 to 6 hours in an oven at 130°-150° F.

CORN SALAD

This plant can be carried over winter in the garden by sowing seed late, in August or September, and mulching the plants with straw or leaves when frost approaches.

ENDIVE

Mulch endive with 6" of straw before the first hard freeze, and it will continue to grow until winter cold really sets in. We have kept it going beyond this point by moving plants to a coldframe. Or, "for winter use," read seedsman advice years ago, "take up before freezing weather, with a large ball of earth attached to the roots, and place in a dry coldframe or cellar, away from frost." The earth should be moist when the plants are lifted.

GARLIC

Harvest and dry garlic as you do onions (see below).

HERBS

Some of the fairly low-growing herbs such as basil, chives, marjoram, mint, parsley, rosemary, and thyme, can be potted and brought indoors for the winter, to grow at a south window; this is most successful when they are being grown in pots sunk in the garden. The way herbs were usually kept for the winter years ago, however, was by drying them, since this provided the quantity needed to see a household through the entire cold season.

The drying was generally simple air drying. "They should be cut on a clear day just before coming into full bloom," went typical directions of the past century, "and dried quickly in the shade. When properly cured, pack them away in tin boxes or bottles, so as to exclude the air." We use this same old method for drying basil, lavender, and mints, but find it convenient to dry other herbs in a 225° F. oven until they are crisp; it takes from 30 minutes to 6 hours, depending on the herbs.

HORSERADISH

Horseradish roots are left in the earth, to be dug as needed during winter. A straw mulch will keep the ground from freezing too hard for digging.

130

Jerusalem
Artichokes

Like horseradish, tubers of Jerusalem artichokes are left in the ground where they grew, and dug as needed. For a convenient supply, bury dug tubers in moist sand in the cellar or keep them in a plastic bag in the refrigerator.

Kale

Like collards, kale is left in the garden for harvest during the winter.

Leeks

Leave leeks in the garden for the winter, with a 6" straw mulch over them.

Lettuce

Lettuce is "stored" for the winter by keeping some growing along under protection. "For a supply in November and December," old advice ran, "plants may be set in a coldframe the last of October and protected with sash when there is danger of freezing." Leaf lettuce is a good choice for this purpose, and should be planted six weeks before it is to be moved to the coldframe—or a coldframe can be dropped over the bed.

Okra

To have okra for winter years ago, it was air dried. The method as given eighty years ago was: "The seed pods when young and tender may be cut in thin slices, strung upon thread, and dried in the shade in the same manner as domestic fruits. When thus cured they may be stored away for winter use." You can dry the pods whole in the oven by blanching them 3 minutes and giving them 3 to 6 hours at 130°-150° F.

Outdoor winter storage of onions, the heap covered with boards and then with earth.

A home-made digger for harvesting onions and some other root crops. A blade section from an old crosscut saw did the digging.

ONIONS

After onions show maturity by turning leaves brownish, bend the leaves over and a few days later pull the onions up, dry them on the ground for another few days if the weather is dry and mild, then store them where it will be cool, airy, and dry during the winter. A cool room temperature will do. Onions used to be braided in strings for this storage; they can be hung in net bags, too. The idea is to give them ventilation.

PARSNIPS

Reliable old advice on winter storage of parsnips was: "Early frosts do not injure the tops or roots and the table qualities are improved by frost. Dig just before the ground freezes up for the winter. Do not cut the roots or trim the tops too closely. Store in a cool, dry cellar, and cover with moist sand." They can also be left in the garden where they grew.

PEPPERS

Peppers can be air dried; hot peppers are usually left whole; sweet peppers can be left whole or cut into ¼″ slices after removing stems and seeds. For oven drying, slice them with a potato peeler and give them 12 to 24 hours at 140°-150° F.

132

POTATOES   Dig your white potatoes when the vines die, brush the tubers clean, and store them in a dry cellar. The temperature is not vital —45° F. to 65° F. will do—but give them air and keep them dark. Loosely piled in a box or barrel covered with a piece of sacking, they will do nicely.

PUMPKINS   Store only well-ripened fruits, and cut them off the vine, leaving a short stem on each fruit. Handle carefully, as cut or bruised fruits will spoil. Old instructions are: "Store in a cool, dry room." The moisture of an outdoor pit will rot pumpkins, and warmth will cause a loss in weight. For best keeping, cure fruits for 10 days at 80° F., then remove them to a dry place with a temperature of 55° F. to 60° F.

RADISHES   Winter radishes can be dug in late fall and stored under cool-moist conditions. Bed them in a box of sand kept moist. In mild-winter climates they can be left in the garden.

RHUBARB   Peter Henderson in 1881 gave the directions for getting fresh rhubarb in winter: "Take large, three- or four-year-old roots from the open field, which if well grown will be fifteen or twenty inches in diameter, and pack them upright as closely as they can be wedged together (with light soil shook in to fill the interstices between the roots) in a warm cellar, say an average of sixty degrees. But little water is needed, and none until the rhubarb shows signs of healthy growth. There is no necessity for light." The season for this forcing was from January to April. Note: roots must go through a low temperature period—freezing or below—before they are brought indoors for forcing. Simply dig them and lay them in a corner of the garden with a mulch over them until they are brought indoors. This breaks their natural dormancy, when freezing weather arrives, and sends them into strong new growth when you bring them indoors for forcing.

SALSIFY

"The roots," read old seedsman instructions, "may be taken up late in autumn and stored in moist sand in a cold room; or they will not be injured if left in the ground and dug when wanted. After growth begins in the spring the roots are unfit for use."

SEA-KALE

Lift roots of sea-kale and force them in the cellar as you do asparagus, but keep them dark. In mild climates they can be forced outdoors by covering the bed with earth and mulch.

SHALLOTS

You dry and store shallots the same way you do onions (see above).

SPINACH

If weekly plantings of spinach are made during September (August in short-summer climates), ran 19th-century advice, "the most forward of these, if covered up with straw at the approach of cold weather will furnish a wholesome vegetable for the table when others are scarce, and the later sowings will withstand the winter with a slight protection of leaves, straw, or other litter."

SQUASH

Winter squashes are handled and stored the way pumpkins are, except acorn squashes, which need no curing before storing.

Summer squashes can be dried for winter by cutting them into slices 1/8" thick, then stringing these on thread. Or the slices can be laid on trays for air drying; they also can be oven dried for 4 to 6 hours at 140°-150° F.

SWEET POTATOES

Here are some good old rules about harvesting sweet potatoes: Determine ripeness beforehand by breaking open several of the sweet potatoes and exposing them to the air. If they keep their color they are ripe and the crop will keep well; if the exposed inner surface turns dark or greenish, they are not yet ripe. If they are ripe, dig them when the ground is dry and before frost comes, after cutting off the vines at ground level and raking them aside. Let the dug sweet potatoes lie exposed to sun and air for a few hours. Cure them by keeping them at 70° F. for two weeks and then transfer to a cooler spot. They can be piled in boxes, and need not be kept in the dark. If any of them have been cut or bruised during harvesting, use these at once, as they will not keep.

TOMATOES

The usual way to store tomatoes in fresh condition is to bring the green ones indoors before frost and lay them on cellar shelves, or cut the plant off near ground level and hang it upside down in the cellar. Either way, the nearest-ripe tomatoes will ripen during the next month or so.

An interesting garden alternative was given by seedsman W. Atlee Burpee in the 1890s: "For a very late crop in localities where there is no frost before the first of November, seed early in June. The first picking will be the latter part of September, and they will be in full bearing two weeks later. At the approach of frost the plants will be loaded with full-sized fruits just beginning to put on the whitish tinge—the first indication of ripening. In a warm situation, with northern protection, dig a trench wide and long enough to contain the plants, which should be cut quite close to the ground. Spread out the plants with their green fruit in the trench until about two feet thick, and over them place a covering of straw six inches in depth, which hold in place by the use of some light brush. The warmth from the earth will ripen the larger fruits perfectly." The trench should be about 30" deep; for a rain-shed it can be covered with two boards set on edge in an inverted V-shape.

Tomatoes can also be dried. Dip ripe fruits in boiling water, peel, slice ¼" thick, dry on trays for 4 to 6 hours at 140°-160° F.

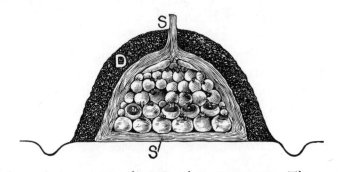

Outdoor winter storage of turnips, beets, or carrots. The roots are surrounded with straw 1"-2" thick, with a vent hole at the top. Six inches of earth are added, and drainage ditches dug.

Turnips and Rutabagas

"To have turnips and rutabagas in a fresh, crisp condition during winter," went old advice, "harvest them before hard frosts and keep in a cool cellar or pit in moist sand or loam."

An English gentleman farmer of the 18th century, one J. Anstruther, reported having experimented in outdoor storage of rutabagas. "I had a few pulled in November, 1789," he reported, "and laid on a grass walk in my garden." There they lay exposed to the weather, including "very hard and severe storms of frost and snow," for six weeks, and were as good eating in April as when first pulled, the writer said. Although some American northern winters are more severe than English ones, the experiment speaks well of the rutabaga's keeping qualities.

Garden Seeds

Years ago, all gardeners let some of each crop go to seed, for planting the next season. Some gardeners still do this and are happy with the results. Saving seed is chancy, but it is also interesting, often economical, and occasionally necessary in order to go on having a certain favorite variety of plant.

One thing to keep in mind is that there is no use saving seed from an F_1 hybrid plant, and many plants today are such hybrids, specified in catalogs and on seed packets. The seed from an F_1 will grow quite a different variety—in fact, a new variety—and while this may be interesting, it isn't apt to be what you'll want as a crop.

Another point is that of cross-pollination, for if two varieties grow close enough to cross ($\frac{1}{4}$-mile separation is fairly safe), the seed from either won't grow plants exactly like either parent. The vegetables least apt to cross are beans (except limas), carrots, celery, eggplant, lettuce, okra, peas, and peppers.

Another point—annual and perennial plants will form seed in one season, but biennials take a second year. Biennials include beets, the cabbage family to some extent, carrots to some extent, celery and celeriac, chard, leeks, usually onions, parsley under most conditions, parsnips, and salsify.

Finally, choose your seed plant not by an outstanding fruit it may bear, but by how outstanding the entire plant is.

To save seeds from fruit vegetables (tomatoes, squash, etc.), let a fruit ripen, scrape seeds out onto a board, and dry them in the shade. Let other seeds mature on the plants, and bring seed heads, pods, etc., indoors to finish final drying on sheets of paper.

When seeds are ready for storage, put them in envelopes, label and date the envelopes, then put them in a plastic bag. Drop in a commercial dessicant or a little package of wood ashes folded in a paper towel and Scotch-taped shut, seal the plastic bag and store it in the refrigerator (not the freezer).

Note: also store any surplus bought seed the same way. Seeds of the following plants, however, are not as apt to survive through to the next spring: onions, parsley, parsnips, and salsify.

If well stored, some seeds were thought to improve with age, according to some early seedsmen, as in this comment of the

Seed Cleaning.

This illustration shows the process of cleaning cucumber seed as practiced commercially in the 1890s. The method is essentially the same when done on a home garden scale today, the ripe cucumbers (tomatoes, cantaloupes, etc.) being cut up so that seeds may be removed for drying.

1890s: "Cucumber, as well as melon and squash seeds, are considered best when two or three years old; they run less to vines, and bear earlier and more abundantly."

Before planting saved seeds, you may want to heed the following: Testing for seed viability was especially necessary in early days when a crop loss from dead seeds would be disastrous, and in 1790 this test was recommended: "Immerge them in water, upon cotton; if they are good they will burst and come up in a state of vegetation." You can do the same thing today by folding seeds in a few thicknesses of a facial tissue and keeping it moist in a saucer for a few days.

CHAPTER

SEVEN

How to Grow Early America's Family Needs and Comforts

IT IS almost impossible, at this distance, to place an accurate value on the household garden of generations ago. We have chosen to call it that—a household garden—because of its astonishing breadth of coverage of human requirements. They ranged from the foods and the flavorings we have already covered in previous chapters, to such diverse things as cosmetics, remedies, containers, brooms, cleaners, insect repellents, sachets and perfumes, self-adornments, toys . . . the list is as fascinating as it is long.

In recounting some of these garden-grown articles of household needs and comforts, we have held the hope that today's gardeners will find more than entertainment here. Many of these now long-abandoned crops are ready and willing to be put to use again, and many of us would be the richer for doing so, both in pocket and in satisfaction of achievement. With this in view, we give for each plant mentioned here, if it is a garden plant and not commonly grown, at least one source of seeds or plants, so that anyone who wishes to do so can raise it for himself, climate willing. In some cases the plant also appears in Chapter 4 or Chapter 5, with seed sources given there. Addresses of suppliers will be found in the Appendix.

ABRASIVES

Wheat, which was among the earliest plants raised by American colonists, possessed a peculiar merit aside from that as a food-stuff. When burned, the ashes of the wheat straw made an abrasive something like powdered pumice, useful for polishing marble and some other fine surfaces. If not available locally, wheat can be ordered from Gurney or Metro Myster Farms, Route 1, Box 285, Northampton, Pennsylvania 18067.

The plant horsetail, a wildling, was used, says Johnson, "as a file, in polishing wood, ivory, or even brass," and also "by dairymaids for cleaning pails and other wooden utensils." The variety called greater rough horsetail was so employed, and was reported growing abundantly on the banks of the Missouri River below the Platte, where it was known as rushes.

Another abrasive was the lining of the luffa gourd, when used as a scouring pad for saucepans. The gourd was ripened on the vine (it turns from green to yellow when ripe), then cut open, the seeds removed and the skin stripped off. The inside fiber was then washed and was ready for use. "It is always sweet and clean as long as any part of it is left," said the 1894 Vaughan catalog.

BEVERAGES

COFFEES ∽ Over the years any number of substitutes for coffee have been developed, sometimes because war or distance cut off the supply of real coffee, sometimes to save money, sometimes for health reasons. Chicory is the best known coffee substitute. The Magdeburg variety is grown commercially for this purpose, as it forms a large root; Field and Stokes list it. But regular witloof chicory can be used and is widely available. An old catalog directed: "In the fall, dig the roots, slice them, and dry in an apple evaporator." A 225° F. oven will serve. After drying, store the slices at room temperature. "When required for use," old directions said, "they should be roasted and ground like coffee." Mix one part of the roasted and ground roots with from one to ten parts of ground coffee. The more chicory, the darker and stronger the brew.

Roasted okra seed can be used as a coffee substitute, and was highly esteemed for this purpose years ago when many substitutes and adulterants for coffee were in wide use.

Dandelion roots were used in exactly the same way to make coffee, and so were carrots. Two other unlikely sounding coffee substitutes were cotton seeds and okra seeds. They were parched and then ground, and all-okra coffee was considered by some an excellent brew. If you want to grow your own cotton seeds, Park and Gurney list the plant; it likes a long, warm summer.

DANDELION WINE ∽ Dandelion wine was popular as an easily made drink and one of considerable alcoholic authority. It was made from the dandelion flowers, sugar, and yeast. Lemons or oranges, or both, were added if available, or just the peel. Some makers included a pinch of hops, some liked the spiciness of ginger added, or of stick cinnamon, and herbs such as rosemary or mint could be included. A fairly typical recipe called for simmering two quarts of flowers in four quarts of spring water for half an hour; this was allowed to blend for a day, then strained off into a crock. To this was added four pounds of sugar, two or three sliced and mashed lemons, and the equivalent of one packet of dry yeast. It was stirred daily, kept at room temperature, and strained into bottles when it stopped fermenting. Tight corking was recommended.

TEAS ∽ To make a herb tea of average strength, pour a pint of boiling water over a handful of fresh leaves or ¼ cup of dried ones, and steep for 20 minutes.

Anise seeds made a tea said to be soothing to the stomach as well as aromatic. Bruise a scant tablespoon of the seeds in a mortar, pour a cup of boiling water over them, steep for 5 minutes.

Balm made a lemon-flavored tea, a nice summer beverage. Park lists the seed, Hemlock Hill and Nichols have plants. Look for "lemon balm" if there is no balm listed.

Bee balm was another plant in early American gardens used to make a tea; it has a minty flavor. Hemlock Hill carries plants, and Nichols carries seeds and plants.

Camomile or Chamomile tea, once greatly esteemed, was made by steeping half a dozen of the dried flowers for 10 minutes in a cup of water brought to a boil. De Giorgi, Nichols, and Park carry the seeds.

142

Flowers of clary, related to common sage, made a tea.

Costmary was admired by some for a tea. Dried leaves were usually used.

Mint teas were much used, and peppermint tea was thought to be good for colds.

Sage, although more used for a medicine, also was made into a beverage tea. To us it still tastes more like medicine.

Strawberry leaves were used to make a delicate tea. They make a good drink and can be used fresh or dried for this.

Thyme made an agreeable tea; if you grow the pretty lemon thyme, which has variegated leaves, it makes an interesting tea.

Violet tea was directed to be made with the leaves, but petals were also called leaves centuries ago.

In colonial America it was the custom to blend two or more herbs in the same tea, as well as using them alone. Taste determined the blending, as mint and strawberry leaves, thyme and rosemary, costmary and sage.

WATERS ✑ A beverage idea brought over from Europe was the "water"— a drink flavored with fruit and served cool. Soft and distinctively flavored berry fruits were best, such as strawberries, currants, raspberries, blackberries and the like. Peaches, pears, and apricots were also used but were boiled first. The method was to mash the fruit, add two or three times as much water, sweeten to taste, and strain off the liquid. Those who had lemons could add some juice. Many variations and additions were possible, including perfumes, rum, or cider—hard or soft.

BONNETS

Here is how the ladies used to obtain literally homegrown bonnets, as described in 1879 by a gardener of Memphis, Tennessee. She is talking about the luffa gourd—"or bonnet gourd as they call it in Texas," she said. "It was pulled before it got quite ripe, the skin stripped off by bits, cut open and washed in cold water until all the seeds and pulp are freed. The inside when dried was made into bonnets. I have trimmed straw hats with strips of it."

CANDY

To make candy of rose petals, violet blossoms, or borage flowers, rinse them, then dry them by tossing on paper towels and pressing between the towels. Next dip them one by one in beaten egg white, and sprinkle with sugar. Let them dry on waxed paper, and halfway through, turn them by inverting the sheet of paper over a fresh one, sprinkling them with more sugar. When crisply dry, store in jars with lids. Children love these dainty candies—as did their great-grandmothers when they too were young. Mint leaves are also very nice when prepared in this way, and any of these confections make fetching little decorations on the icing of cupcakes.

CLEANERS

Sponges from lining of the luffa gourd were used to wash dishes, clean vegetables, and wash down woodwork.

In her *Gardening with Herbs*, Helen Morgenthau Fox says that the juice of marjoram was used to clean furniture. The plant contains a volatile oil, resin, and tannin.

The soapwort mentioned later in this chapter as a shampoo was also valued for cleaning delicate fabrics. For this, the leaves were sometimes boiled, to obtain a sudsing washwater.

Brooms and whiskbrooms were made from the reed-like stems of broom corn. A native of India, broom corn came to Europe in 1759 and, Peter Henderson stated, was brought to American attention by Benjamin Franklin. "He is said to have accidentally seen an imported whisk of corn in the possession of a lady of Philadelphia, and while examining it as a curiosity, found a seed, which he planted, and from that single seed has sprung this important article of agriculture and manufacture in the United States."

In his farmer's dictionary Johnson said, "If the stalks are cut before the seed is ripe, they are better, stronger and more durable." The stalks, or stems, were then spread in a sheltered, airy place to dry. A good broom took about 1½ pounds of the stems, and was tied with either cord or wire. A rustic broom suitable for fireplace use and also handy for general sweeping can be made by merely fastening a bundle of stems around a stick. Gather the stems a third of the way down with a few turns of cord, and secure the cord by threading another length of it through the broom and around the wound cord at three or four points. Gurney carries broom corn seed.

CONTAINERS

Yesterday's household grew a great many of its everyday articles simply by planting a few gourd vines. You can sow the seeds of these same gourds today and make the same useful articles. Besides, the gourds form an attractive and often fragrant vine screen during the summer, as for shade on the side of a porch, and the flowers are quite ornamental. Here is the word from the 1887 Burpee catalog as to gourds:

"Sugar trough gourds are useful for many household purposes such as buckets, baskets, nest-boxes, soap and salt dishes, and for storing the winter's lard. They grow to hold from four to ten gallons each, have thick, hard shells, very light but durable, having been kept in use as long as ten years."

The sugar-trough gourd is a pear shape and grows to such heroic size that households of years ago used the mature, dried gourds to hold up to 10 gallons of lard—enough to last the winter. Today the gourds still make splendid containers for various household uses such as wastebaskets, firewood holders, vegetable bins, etc.

Dippers and birdhouses were made from the dipper gourd, spoons were made from the spoon gourd or it was left whole to form a darning egg for stockings or to become a rattle for the baby because of the dried seeds inside. Dippers and spoons made from gourds had the advantage of handles that stayed cool when dealing with hot liquids.

This old catalog illustration is one of the nest-egg gourd, which so closely resembled a hen's egg, it was placed in the nests to set an example.

The nest-egg gourd grew egg-like fruits, used in nests to en-

146

courage hens. "We had a vine of the egg gourd," an Illinois gardener stated in 1886, "that bore fruit so natural that I think it would have deceived the old hen herself."

The genus of gourds called Langenaria are the ones that produce the hard-shelled and long-lasting fruits. They should be planted when weather is warm, or started indoors in short-summer climates. (Tip from the 1850s: "If, after a few gourds have set, the ends are pinched off the vines, the gourds will grow larger and better.") Harvest fruits before frost and when fully ripe, handling carefully to avoid bruising. Then with a sharp knife slice away the unwanted parts, to form the container, dipper, or whatever. Remove seeds, wash the gourd with a strong household disinfectant, and put it in a dry and ventilated place. Turn it every few days while drying, which will take weeks and in some cases months. You can polish it with paste wax or coat it with shellac when completely dried, although no coating is necessary for preservation.

The 1893 catalog of Vaughan's Seed Store showed the luffa gourd in use as a washcloth—by a Japanese man, since the plant was identified here as coming from Japan.

Other uses that were made of gourds as holders were as kitchen bins for grains and root vegetables, as sewing baskets, as pencil holders, and for waste baskets; also for holding paper spills to ignite lamps, candles, and firewood, and as holders for pine cones at the hearth to start the fire.

Nearly every seed house today carries gourds, even though some list them among flowers. Park has an excellent listing.

COSMETICS

The versatile luffa gourd was also used to make washcloths and bath sponges. (For preparing the lining, see Abrasives.) Interestingly, the luffa sponge is still sold commercially in spite of heavy competition from synthetic sponges. Many drug stores sell luffa sponges for about $2 each, showing how well it pays to raise your own.

Saponaria officinalis, commonly called soapwort or Bouncing Bet, is a showy flowering plant that grows so readily it can become a weed. But its great virtue is its sudsing quality, for its bruised leaves act as a soap when agitated in water, and the lather can be used as a shampoo. Nichols lists saponaria among its herb plants.

Sorrel leaves were used as a hand bleach in years past, the juice removing some stains. De Giorgi and Nichols list sorrel.

Nineteenth century belles found that a freshly cut beet provided a cheek rouge—as anyone who handles beets would agree to. The red juice is a temporary skin dye.

Sesame seeds, popular in cookies, were also a source of a cosmetic in days past. The seeds were also known as bene, benne, or benny, and it was their oil that was the cosmetic, used to soften and whiten the skin. You can grow sesame easily in the subtropical South; elsewhere start plants ahead of time, like tomatoes, and hope you'll have a long-enough warm summer to ripen seeds. To extract their oil, seeds were bruised in a mortar, hot water was poured over them, and the oil that came to the top was

148

skimmed off. The oil keeps exceptionally well. De Giorgi lists sesame.

Another oil treatment for the skin was one known for centuries, an oil of roses. It was made by steeping rose petals in a bland oil. You can use mineral oil. If a sufficient quantity of rose petals were put into a crock, covered with water, and put in a warm place, old advice ran, a little oil would rise to the surface; it was collected on a piece of dry cotton wool and then squeezed into a bottle. This was attar of roses, the rare and costly fragrance. Another collecting method was to chill the water, congealing the oil so that it could be picked up like bits of butter.

To make rose water, which was produced for use as a delicate perfume or a refreshing lotion, do this: Put 6 cups of fresh rose petals and water to cover them in a large aluminum or enameled saucepan. Simmer for 2 or 3 hours. The water that remains will become the rose water after you strain the mixture through a muslin bag as if you were making jelly. Discard the pulp and store the rose water in a stoppered bottle.

The herb costmary was boiled in water to produce an aromatic face wash.

Cucumbers were made into a skin lotion much favored by ladies of yesterday. The recipes usually called for a simple and short cooking and straining, and flower petals were often added for their fragrance. A typical recipe called for simmering 2 quarts of full-blown rose petals for an hour in water to cover them, then adding a finely minced cucumber (or put it through a blender) and simmering for another 10 minutes. Strain off the liquid. A tablespoon of lemon juice could be added but was not usually available in early days. The lotion was smoothed on the face and neck for a few minutes before washing or bathing.

A somewhat similar lotion was made from strawberries, and was reputed good for clearing the complexion.

NEW GIANT WHITE CUCUMBER.

We have never seen handsomer cucumbers than those grown at FORDHOOK FARM of this very distinct and valuable new variety. The cucumbers are of gigantic size and always of a *pure waxen white*, from the time they are are first set until matured. They grow from twelve to sixteen inches long by from two to three inches in diameter, very uniform, straight, and perfectly smooth. The flesh is very solid, pure white, with exceptionally few seeds, and is exceedingly crisp, of *most superior flavor*. As a variety for slicing they will prove very useful, while for exhibition no other cucumber will attract so much attention. We measured a magnificent specimen grown in our trial grounds the past season, *nearly seventeen inches long by three and a quarter inches in diameter*, that *weighed six and a quarter pounds*,—so very solid and heavy are the fruits of the GIANT WHITE, while the *pure waxen white color* is extremely attractive. The foliage is large and luxuriant ; the fruits are borne near the hill.

This GIANT WHITE Cucumber should not be confounded with the Long Chinese nor with the Ivory Monarch,—varieties recently introduced by other houses. The former is of weak, delicate constitution, and many of the cucumbers are green, while the latter is badly malformed,—all the fruits produced in our trial grounds being compressed in the middle. The GIANT WHITE is therefore the first and only first-class LONG White Cucumber yet introduced.

Per pkt. 10 cts.; 3 pkts. for 25 cts.; per oz. 50 cts.

NEW GIANT WHITE CUCUMBER.

BURPEE'S GIANT PERA CUCUMBER.

THE GIANT PERA is a most prolific variety ; the cucumbers are set early, near the hill, and very close together. As shown in the illustration, the cucumbers uniformly grow very smooth and straight; the skin is a beautiful medium green, perfectly smooth, free from spines, and retains its clear green color until nearly ripe. They are very thick through, perfectly round, full at the blossom end, and of equal diameter throughout, except that they taper a little at the stem end. The green cucumbers are fit to eat at any stage, the flesh is *entirely white, very clear, peculiarly crisp, tender* and *brittle*, with *very few seeds*, and free from the obnoxious "green cucumber taste." The seed cavity is remarkably small, and the seeds are so slow to form that even large cucumbers, twelve to fifteen inches in length and three inches in diameter, are still equally as firm and crisp as smaller specimens, the seeds being yet almost unformed. A mature Giant Pera eighteen to twenty-two inches long will hardly give as much seed as a small, short green cucumber.

Per pkt. 10 cts.; per oz. 20 cts.; ¼ ℔ 60 cts.; per ℔ $2.00.

BURPEE'S WHITE PEARL.

Our crops of this new Cucumber have been the admiration of seedsmen and gardeners. One grower for market, from Boston, Mass., said : "It is the cucumber I have been looking for all my life, but never expected to see. I never ate a finer cucumber." In habit of growth it is entirely distinct, setting the cucumbers very close around the stem, and maturing these early, then afterward the vines continue to run and bear freely throughout the season. The cucumbers grow so thickly together that they actually lie piled one upon the other. They grow remarkably uniform ; the skin is very smooth and entirely free from spines. In color they are a *beautiful pearly white ;* even the young fruits are of a very light color, nearly as pure white as when ready for use.

Per pkt. 10 cts.; 3 pkts. for 25 cts.; per oz. 35 cts.

BURPEE'S GIANT PERA CUCUMBER.

ENTERTAINMENT

For those who disapproved of tobacco, or didn't have any, dried leaves of sage were available and were said to be an acceptable substitute. Another combination was catnip and clover, and most boys of past generations were familiar with cornsilk as a smoke. Tobacco was well known in Europe before there was any considerable colonization of America, and most Indian tribes were well acquainted with tobacco, mainly in ceremonial usage, as in pledges of friendship. (For tobacco culture see Chapter 3.)

Corncob dolls were enchanting little toys for children in colonial days and later, and can easily be made. After shelling off the corn, dry the cob with the shucks left on. Then pull the shucks up and back for the "hair." Slit them and make them into braids, or curl them this way: hold a strip of slit shuck between thumb and a knife blade and pull the shuck strip through, just as tie-ribbon is curled. Cobs from midget corn make especially charming tiny dolls, also nice for decorations.

FRAGRANCES

Costmary was valued for its minty smell, used dried to lend a grateful aroma to linen presses, bed clothing, and the like.

Dried flowers of lavender were also much liked for the nice fragrance they gave to clothing and linens, and the flowers and seeds went into sachets. Lavender is a perennial, grown from seeds, cuttings, or root divisions. It likes a light side dressing of wood ashes in the spring.

A little melon that was grown for its fragrance is Queen Anne's pocket melon, or pomegranate melon. Related to the cantaloupe, it is botanically *Cucumis melo*, var. *dudaim*. Al-

LEFT: *Cucumbers figured in some home-made beauty preparations years ago, making the fruit one of the garden's multi-purpose vegetables.*

though not edible, this pretty little ball-shaped fruit, striped and mottled yellow over orange, smelled so good that ladies carried it with them like a pomander ball, and displayed it in their homes for its beauty and perfume. Give it the same culture as cantaloupes. Seed is carried by Park, among gourds.

Roses in the old gardens were for more than bouquets. The fragrant petals were used as already mentioned, and if put with some other ingredients in a potpourri, could perfume an entire room. To make a potpourri you will need a pint-sized glass or pottery jar with a lid, and these ingredients: Four lightly packed cups of fresh rose petals, 3 tablespoons of mixed spices such as ground cloves and allspice, and a tablespoon of powdered orris root from the drug store or about ¼ cup of dried clary leaves (see Chapter 4 for clary). Air dry the petals on paper towels until crisp; about three summer days should do it, and you can dry them in batches until you have enough, stockpiling them in the jar as you go. Then sprinkle the other ingredients over them, stir gently but well, and put the lid on the jar. Open it whenever you want the fragrance to escape. It should last at least a year. There were all sorts of recipes for potpourris, as if anything that smelled good was a candidate—other flowers, sweet herbs, fragrant grasses, vanilla, lemon and orange rind, walnut leaves, and so on.

HOME DECORATION
The household garden supplied an interesting range of things for decorating homes years ago, and still does for gardeners who realize the possibilities. One curious plant no longer seen much is the martynia (described in Chapter 4). When seeds mature they develop into bird-like forms. The best use we know of for these is as Christmas tree ornaments. An artist friend in Big Sur, California, painted the pods a flat white, sprinkling them with a pinch of glitter while the paint was still wet, then hung them on the tree later with metal thread. Another artist made a mobile of the birds, painting each a different color.

Ornamental corn and the more colorful among gourds have been used as fall decorations for generations. The tiny popcorn called Strawberry is effective for this, too, and can be popped afterward.

In an August issue of a gardening magazine of the 19th century a reader advised that "now is the time to begin gathering grasses for winter bouquets. Set a box of dry sand in a dark place and stick the stems of the grasses in the sand." This way, the grasses looked more natural when dried, the writer explained, than if hung head down to dry. Everlasting flowers, as seed catalogs call them, are still grown to form winter bouquets. Some of them are armeria, bells of Ireland, celosia, centaurea, Chinese lantern, gypsophila, larkspur, lunaria, statice, and strawflowers. The simple way to dry them is: Cut them before they are full-blown, strip off any leaves, and hang them head down in a cool, shady, and mildly airy place until they feel dry. Another method, suggested by the Harris seed company, is to put the flower stems in a solution of one part glycerine and two parts water. A third way is to cover the flowers with a dessicant until they are dry. Two brand names are Flower-Dri, and Dryonex. Seed catalogs often list one of these among their everlasting flower group.

Besides using the dried flowers in bouquets, gardeners have shown ingenuity with such other uses as in shadow-box pictures, in glass lamp bases, and to decorate gift packages.

Another way flowers were preserved was by pressing. A friend, Miss Beatrice C. Howitt, with a distinguished career in science, is by avocation a botanist, and she gives the following procedure that she uses when pressing plants or flowers:

> The plant is put immediately on a sheet of newspaper and the sheet is folded over it. On top of the newspaper is placed a sheet of heavy blotting paper and then a sheet of grocery-carton cardboard. For convenience, each of the

layers—newspaper sheet, blotting paper, and cardboard—is precut to a size that will fit whatever plant press is used. The whole thing is then put in the plant press (a simple frame with clamps or straps to exert pressure on the contents), and the press is put in a warm place such as near a water heater. There it remains for up to a week; it should be turned twice a day for evener drying, and the newspaper is replaced with fresh newspaper once or twice, particularly if the plant was .quite moist when the pressing was begun. The faster the drying, the better are colors retained. When dry, the pressed plant can be mounted on mounting paper with paste or adhesive straps.

This method was used years ago to make albums of pressed flowers, and some interesting pictures were made in the same way. A more modern use has been to mount pressed specimens between sheets of clear plastic or glass, as for a window or a free-standing screen.

INSECT REPELLENTS

To keep insects away from one while outdoors, camomile tea was dabbed on the exposed skin.

For keeping moths out of clothes chests, sprigs of rosemary or wormwood were put into the chests.

Several plants were believed to be effective insect chasers when sprigs of them were hung or otherwise displayed in rooms. Among these plants were sage and tansy, to chase flies; spearmint for the same purpose; rue to repel flies, fleas, and some other insects; and pennyroyal to discourage flies, mosquitoes, and other pests. Pennyroyal's name, in fact, says this, for "penny" is a corruption of the Latin *pulex* for flea, and "royal" meant a relief or defense. Johnny and Nichols list pennyroyal, and the other plants mentioned are available from many seedsmen.

154

JEWELRY "Beads" from the garden have long been provided by colorful seeds such as from ornamental corn, sunflowers, castor beans, and Job's tears plants. But rose-petal beads with their sweet, mild fragrance, have been especially well liked. To make them you will need an iron skillet and enough rose petals to firmly pack a measuring cup three times. Put the petals in the skillet with just enough water to cover them, and simmer gently, uncovered, for two or three hours, stirring a few times. Let the mixture cool, and repeat the cooking each day during the next few days until you have a dryish cooked-down pulp. To make the beads, roll spoonfuls of this pulp between your palms to form balls. Dry the balls at room temperature by threading them on waxed dental floss with a darning needle. Thumbtack each end of the floss to opposite sides of a window frame and let the beads dry; it will take about a week; turn each of them a few times and keep them from sticking to each other during this drying. They can be left on the floss or restrung with glass or china beads between them to add interest. A devout Roman Catholic friend made rose beads into rosaries for gifts; handling the beads gives one's fingers a light rose fragrance.

Another old procedure for making the beads is simpler. The rose petals are worked into a paste with mortar and pestle, then rolled into pea-sized balls and strung on silk thread before they become dry and hard. The perfume was said to last for a generation.

MISCELLANEOUS An interesting secondary use of the globe artichoke was given by Johnson in his 1851 farmer's encyclopedia: "The flowers of the artichoke have the property of rennet in curdling milk."

REMEDIES Thrown upon their own resources, early American gardeners relied heavily on treatments of ills with plants from

155

their own gardens and from the countryside. As a result, as Anne Leighton says in her very readable *Early American Gardens*, "the practice of medicine in seventeenth century New England became the first flourishing home industry." And its practice continued into the centuries that followed, even experiencing a revival of interest in the last decade.

Some plants in times gone by were selected for pretty thin reasons; the lungwort, for example, was thought to be good for lung troubles because the leaves look like an outline of the lungs. Many plant medicines were soundly chosen, however, as science later discovered. Foxglove, to take one instance, was once used to treat dropsy—and is the source of digitalis, the heart medicine. But herb doctoring had to be done with skill, especially if the dose was swallowed. Overdoses of foxglove or pennyroyal, to name two, have been fatal. Moderation is extremely important in the dosing with herbs, which may be much stronger than they seem.

The rule for gathering herbs was to do so as they were starting to bloom. If they were to be stored for winter they were air dried in the shade, then put into cloth bags. Jars or cans may be used also.

BALM ✑ To produce sweating, thought to be a help in ridding the body of ills, a tea was made of balm leaves.

A gargle for a sore throat was made by mashing balm leaves, steeping them in vinegar, then straining off the vinegar and stirring in a little honey.

RIGHT: *Citizens of the 19th century were bombarded with patent "cures" for nearly every ill that flesh was heir to, but many of them preferred old herbal remedies their ancestors had used.*

156

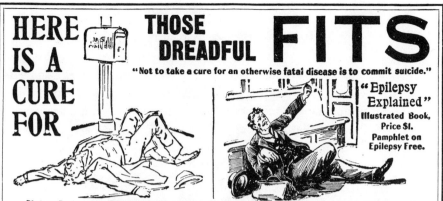
CHILDREN'S CORNER.

Dear Mr. Park:—I am a little girl ten years old. I have two sisters and three brothers Their names are Effie, Daisy, Walter, Jimmie and Freddy. My mamma takes your Magazine. I like to read it. She received the flower seeds you sent her. I like them very well. I planted some Poppy seeds. I enjoy the letters children write to you and I thought I would write.

Lona Vilitoe.

Jackson Co., Onio, Apr. 23, 1898.

Dear Mr. Park:—I am a little girl seven years old. My mamma takes your Magazine. I like to read the letters from the children. Both of my grandmas got lovely flowers from you. I love flowers very much. There are some very pretty wild flowers in the woods near our house. My choice is the beautiful Wood Lily.

Anna May Drake.

Athens Co., Ohio, Apr. 26, 1898.

Dear Mr. Park:—Mamma said I might write for the Children s Corner. I am a little girl ten years old. I go to school every day. Papa built us a new house last summer, and mamma says she must have Park's 10-cent collection of flower seeds to plant in the front yard. I have three sisters and two brothers. My youngest sister is three months old. I think she will love flowers for she takes more notice of our house plants than of any thing else. She has blue eyes and very thick, long brown hair. Her name is Doris.

Winnie Erickson.

Renville Co., Minn., Mar. 23, 1898.

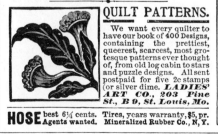

BALSAM APPLE ∾ A gourd, the balsam apple (*Momordica balsamina*) found a use years ago as a wound healer. It is a yellowish-orange egg-shaped fruit which, according to an old materia medica, was "soaked in whisky and used domestically as a vulnerary," or application to cuts. Seeds of the balsam apple are carried by Park, and by Stokes as "wild cucumber."

The dried blossoms of calendula, also called pot marigold, were used during the Civil War to treat bruises and sprains.

CALENDULA ∾ The dried flowers of this pretty annual were put to medical use as an antiseptic in the form of a tincture of bruised leaves and alcohol. This appeared in older U.S. materia medicas and is said to have been used during the Civil War. Seedsman Peter Henderson noted that the tincture was considered "highly efficacious for bruises or sprains."

CANNA ∾ In 1877 a lady in West Virginia wrote *Park's Floral Magazine* to say the canna was called "the headache weed" in Florida. "The leaf," she reported, "wilted a little and bound on the forehead

The popular lawn flower, canna, had a name in some parts of the country a century ago for serving as a headache treatment. The broad leaves were applied to the aching forehead.

would relieve a person's headache. My sister tried it last summer, and said as soon as she put it on that her head became moist and got better immediately.''

CATNIP A tea of catnip was also considered a headache cure, as well as a stimulant and tonic. It is also an agreeable drink. Bruised catnip leaves were once used to quiet toothache pain and to relieve hemorrhoids. Catnip also had a name as an aphrodisiac, but apparently only among cats. Our own experience is, it puts cats to sleep and is a good multi-purpose medicine for them.

CELERY ↝ Celery was once considered decidedly a medical plant, not a table one. It was thought effective in relieving rheumatism, aiding digestion, and as a stimulant. A tea was made of the seeds, for rheumatism.

CHERVIL ↝ As a treatment for bruises, dried chervil was moistened with water and bandaged on.

CHICORY ↝ Johnson said the juice of chicory root was "slightly tonic; and has been used in chronic affections of the stomach, connected with torpid liver."

COMFREY ↝ Comfrey root was boiled in water or wine, and the liquid taken as a medicine for various ills. Recent investigations reported by the Henry Doubleday Research Association in Essex, England, indicate that comfrey is the only plant that contains lantoin, a substance that increases the body's number of white blood corpuscles. If so, comfrey's name as a disease fighter may stem from this. Gurney, Hemlock Hill, and Nichols list comfrey plants.

DANDELION ↝ The dandelion had a good name as a many-purpose medicine in early days. Johnson said: "It is a valuable medicine, is aperient, powerfully diuretic," and that it tended to change the bodily condition to a normal state, was good for liver complaints, but that its use should be omitted for a few days now and then as it was apt to derange the stomach. The medical properties were affirmed by old materia medicas, which specified the dried root of the dandelion, gathered in the fall, as the part to use, noting that it was known to the Arabians as a blood purifier.

GARLIC ✍ After its introduction into English gardens in the mid-16th century, garlic became highly valued as a medicine and famous for its odor. Peter Henderson called the odor "far more diffusive and penetrating than that of the onion. So powerful that when garlic is applied to the feet the smell is said to be observed in the breath and perspiration." Garlic was an official drug in the United States pharmacopoeia from 1820 to 1900. The cloves were used fresh, both internally and in poultices, for various troubles from insect stings and snake bites to abscesses, indigestion, and bronchitis. In earlier times, garlic was eaten to kill worms in the alimentary tract. We have fed it to our dogs for that purpose, and had a veterinary's word for its effectiveness against certain worms.

HOREHOUND ✍ Horehound leaves were cooked in water until the liquid was reduced to a well-flavored residue, of which a syrup was made with sugar. When cooked to the candying stage, this became horehound cough drops. The leaves also made a tea, given for relief of coughs, for rheumatism, and as a laxative.

HYSSOP ✍ A tea of hyssop leaves was given for chest colds, and hyssop was in old materia medicas as useful for bronchitis, sore throat, and chronic catarrhs. The plant was also considered effective in treating rheumatism and bruises, presumably by local applications. (See Chapter 5 for sources.)

LAVENDER ✍ A tea made from the flowers of the lavender plant was taken for the nerves. The tea was also used to promote sneezing, perhaps by snuffing it up the nostrils. As a drink the tea was also considered a mild stimulant.

MARJORAM ✍ Although oregano was the usual plant here, marjoram was a substitute for it, and marjoram is more often found in gardens. A tea was made of the leaves to sooth the stomach and also to help neuralgia and rheumatism. An oil in the plant was used medically years ago in liniments.

MINT ∽ Bruised mint leaves were applied to stings, to ease pain.

ONIONS ∽ A poulice of crushed roasted onions boiled with neatsfoot oil was used by early colonists for gout and sciatica pains. A neighbor recently told us of how her Norwegian grandfather, when she was a little girl, used to treat her earache with a drop of onion juice and a plug of cotton.

RHUBARB ∽ Ordinary rhubarb was popularly regarded as a spring tonic and laxative, good for you after the long winter without fresh green vegetables was finally over.

ROSE ∽ Rose conserve was one of the valued remedies for many complaints in colonial days. These included colds, digestive upsets, and ulcers of the mouth. A lotion was made for chapped skin and burns. One way of making the conserve was by working in a mortar equal amounts by weight of rose petals and sugar, moistened with rose water or honey to form a paste. Another formula called for stewing rose petals in a little water, straining, and boiling with honey. The Provence rose was considered best.

A treatment for headaches was vinegar of roses, made by soaking dried petals in white vinegar. The fluid was dabbed on the forehead or used to moisten a cloth laid over the head.

ROSEMARY ∽ The neat and lovely rosemary with its tiny blue flowers and leaves so like evergreen needles, has been famous for centuries as a healing plant. A tea was made of it for coughs and general well-being. The boiled leaves were applied to gouty legs. An ointment was made by extracting the oil from the leaves through pounding them with a little sweet oil in a mortar. By incorporating this with melted petroleum jelly we have made an ointment for scratches and cuts. The ancient Saxons made similar use of a rosemary ointment.

SAGE ✍ Sage came to America with centuries-old reputation for benefiting human health and conferring long life. There are wonderful tales of very old villagers in England who had made a lifelong habit of growing and using sage. Old materia medicas noted sage tea's value as a gargle for sore throats and to relieve nasal catarrh. An oil in the leaves is the medical factor. A cough syrup was made by adding honey and vinegar to sage tea; a teaspoonful was a dose, and the amounts of each ingredient were determined by the maker.

SAVORY ✍ Summer and winter savory used to be made into teas for the relief of digestive troubles, among other things. We have found no corroboration of their effectiveness in old materia medicas, however.

SESAME ✍ The leaves of sesame were used to treat dysentery. Peter Henderson gave the recipe: "A dozen leaves put in a tumbler of water quickly give out a mucilaginous, starch-like substance, in which condition it can be freely used." De Giorgi lists sesame.

SOAPWORT ✍ The soapwort (*Saponaria*) that cleaned delicate fabrics and shampooed hair, was also used by early Americans against the rash caused by poison ivy, presumably to wash the skin. If done soon after exposure to poison ivy it would probably have been helpful.

164

TANSY ∽ A liniment made by steeping tansy leaves in alcohol was used externally for bruises, sprains, and rheumatism. Hemlock Hill and Nichols list plants.

THYME ∽ A volatile oil, thymol, in thyme has anesthetic and antiseptic properties, as reported in materia medicas. Thyme was used in baths, and—most probably as a tea—for skin eruptions, muscular rheumatism, and flatulence. Thyme was also used to relieve toothache; a moist pack of chewed leaves was a common way of treating toothache.

TOBACCO ∽ Tobacco, like lavender, was used to encourage sneezing, thought to be a healthy habit and also valued as an antidote to some fits. A pinch of powdered tobacco was snuffed up the nostrils. Snuff was probably the preferred form, although homegrown tobacco rubbed to a powder would serve.

TOMATO ∽ In the mid-19th century the tomato, then slowly coming into favor as a food, ranked also as a remedy. Johnson described it this way: "The juice is cooling to the system, and is applied externally to remove eruptions upon the skin."

VINEGARS

As preservatives and for flavoring, vinegars played an active role in the homes of years past. A second stage, or by-product, of wine and some other alcoholic drinks, vinegars were of various kinds, and many were flavored additionally with herbs. To do this, drop up to half a dozen sprigs of the herb into a bottle of white vinegar. Good choices are basil, marjoram, spearmint, tarragon, and thyme.

A 19th-century recipe for a homemade vinegar directed: "An excellent vinegar for domestic purposes may be readily made by exposing a mixture of one part of brown sugar by weight with seven parts of water and some yeast, in a cask whose bung-hole is only slightly covered over (as by a piece of gauze pasted down to keep out insects), for some weeks to the action of the atmosphere and the sun. The acetic fermentation and the goodness of the vinegar are promoted by the addition of vine leaves." Leaves of a grape vine were meant here.

YEAST

In old days, yeast came partly from the garden. This recipe was printed in 1794 but dated back some years before that:

"Boil potatoes of the mealy sort till they are thoroughly soft; skin and mash them very smooth, and put as much hot water as will make the mash of the consistency of common beer yeast, but not thicker. Add to every pound of potatoes two ounces of coarse sugar, and when just warm, stir in for every pound of potatoes two spoonfuls of yeast. Keep it warm till it has done fermenting, and in 24 hours it may be used. A pound of potatoes will make near a quart of yeast, and when made will keep three months. Lay your bread eight hours before you bake it."

Another way of making yeast was with hops. (See Chapter 4 for hop culture.) The hops (dried cones of the female flowers) were boiled in potato water. This was cooled, then a little yeast from a previous batch was added, and the mixture was allowed to ferment.

EIGHT

Old Ways with Flowers for Today

THE flower garden has been a cherished part of household gardening in America during the past two centuries. Although grim necessity had to come first in the very first gardens of the New World, flowers for flowers' sake quickly followed. And when the westward trek began, flower seeds were squeezed into jammed storage quarters of the pioneer wagons, to spread their delicate beauty across the continent.

In this chapter we take you on a browsing visit to some gardens of bygone amateur florists, as hobby flower growers called themselves years ago. We have selected a handful of popular flowers to talk about—most of them still widely grown—and another handful of flower-growing activities. It is a kind of eavesdropping visit, a listening to voices of generations ago talking of their flower loves and fancies, yet shot through with surprisingly timely and practical advice.

Following the flowers themselves, the order of arrangement is alphabetical under the headings: Arranging Plants in Beds;

167

Cuttings, Frost Protection, Garden Etiquette, Gardenless Garden, Hanging Baskets, House Plants, Perennials, Planters, Potting, Tussie-Mussies, and Wardian Cases.

This type of sprinkling can was being used a century ago. The long spout made it convenient to reach potted plants.

ALYSSUM

The modest little sweet alyssum, perennial in mild climates, has been prized by gardeners for a long time. "The flowers are not large," an old seedsman told his customers, "but are borne in clusters and are valued for their delicate fragrance." One trouble the plant was having in those days was a so-called black flea, and a remedy was to sow seed indoors, as the insect was less troublesome to transplants. Another counter-measure was to sprinkle plants with wood ashes or slaked lime in the early morning.

One year when we had Martha Washington geraniums on a deck, it happened that some alyssum seed sprouted in the pots. We let the plants remain and were rewarded by an avalanche of honey-smelling white blossoms. There were several linnets about, and one pair came daily to nestle in the pots and eat the forming seeds. Since then we have put two or three alyssum plants around larger pot plants. The Violet Queen variety is charming with a Cecile Brunner rose; white alyssums can be had in both tall and dwarf plants.

168

To have alyssum blooming indoors in winter, a gardener of years ago suggested lifting thrifty young plants in August and potting them. "By November they will commence blooming," the reader was assured, "and furnish you with abundance of delicate flowers." Alyssum is an annual. Its perennial relatives are known as madworts ("mad" for anger, "wort" for plant) for their supposed ability to soothe rage.

BALSAM

It was once more the custom than it is now to train even small plants as miniature espaliers. Here is a gardener of the 1870s describing such handling with the pretty little annual, balsam: "It may by judicious training be made to assume almost any shape. Some train them to one branch by pinching off the side shoots, thus making them grow tall and slender; others prefer to leave three or five shoots. In either case the plant is very handsome and if properly cared for will be a mass of bloom."

Another comment on balsam from this same period was: "It is half hardy, and like the aster needs a rich soil, sunny position, and plenty of water."

FUCHSIAS

Here is some old advice on how to train a fuchsia, a half-hardy annual, to grow on a little trellis. We have done this training with Cecile Brunner rose and nasturtiums—though using bamboo supports, not hoopskirt wires: "When a fuchsia slip has grown six or eight inches high, pinch out the top down to the last set of leaves. It will then throw out branches on each side. Let those grow eight or ten inches, then pinch out as before; again pinch the tops of each branch when grown the same height as the others. Procure a stick the size of your finger, eighteen inches in length; take a hoopskirt wire and twine back and forth alternately through holes made in the stick equal distances apart. Place this firmly in the pot back of the plant, tie the branches to it, and you will have when in flower a beautiful and very graceful plant."

This word was passed along by a Kansas gardener in the

The graceful fuchsia with its bell-like flowers was a favorite house plant in cold-weather climates years ago.

1870s: "Fuchsias are very sensitive to sun shining on the pot they are grown in. Many in the Old Country who have choice fuchsias sink the pot into another pot about two inches larger, and fill in with earth. Watering them with water that salt beef or pork has been boiled in helps them. They like a moist atmosphere, and do not do well in Kansas, it is so dry. Summer fuchsias will keep well in a cellar during winter without water. When brought out in the spring looking dry as sticks, they will soon show leaves."

GLADIOLAS

Culture of gladiolas, half-hardy perennials, is still a moot subject, as it was a century ago, when a professional nurseryman detailed: "I throw out the earth to the depth of 18 inches, and fill in with 12 inches of fine dirt or leafmold mixed with one third of sand or other coarse soil. On this I place the bulbs and fill up with any good soil. By this culture I grow them from 6 to 8 feet high. When I take them up in the fall I let the tops dry on the bulbs before I cut them off. The small bulbs that form between the old and the new will not grow if planted the next spring, but if kept a year longer they will grow as strongly and surely as potatoes."

Exception to some of the points was quickly taken by another gardener. His gladiolas, he said, grew no taller than four feet; and as for the small bulbs—"I have been planting them by the tens and hundreds, and only a very few fail to grow the next spring."

HYACINTHS

The problem of hyacinths that fail to bloom was worrying gardeners long ago, as it worries some today. One lady advised her sister gardeners: "I have a remedy . . . and I do feel a little surprised that it is not generally known that a piece of stiff paper twisted in the shape of a cornucopia, or funnel-shaped, with an inch opening at the top to admit light, inverted over the leaves of the bulb in the pot so as not to exclude the light from the crown of the bulb, will obviate the difficulty and cause the stem to elongate itself so as to reach the light, and a fine display of blooms will be the result." A possibly more experienced gardener remarked: "When hyacinths fail to throw up the spikes to the usual height, it is because they have been brought to the light before the roots were properly developed." The plant is a perennial.

This note about rooting hyacinth leaves appeared in an 1877 newspaper: "The leaves of the hyacinth, cut off near the bulb, will make new bulbs as geranium leaves do."

LILY-OF-THE-VALLEY

A bit of old advice from an Illinois gardener on lily-of-the-valley, a perennial, is worth repeating today: "Lily-of-the-valley should have rich soil, be kept clean from weeds when it comes up in the spring, and be *let alone* otherwise. It is a hardy flower. To have it in winter, get the 'pips'; or it can sometimes be chopped out of the ground in January, brought into the house, and forced." A lily-of-the-valley pip is a rooted bud that arises from the rootstock, and is what is usually planted to start a new bed.

171

An old bed will provide plenty of such pips. To force pips, lift some at the end of summer, then plant them any time in pots filled with sand. Keep them dark and moist for two weeks, then bring them into the light for growth and flowering. To get flowers by Christmas, professional Dutch growers of the 1870s planted moss-wrapped pips in sand about a month ahead of Christmas and gave them bottom heat and liberal watering until sprouts appeared.

LOBELIA

One of the nice things about the pretty little lobelia, usually grown as an annual, is its willingness to do its best, and even to self-seed, as this 19th-century gardener testified: "One of the prettiest little house plants is the lobelia, a plant one can have all the time without renewing. Three years ago I sowed some seed, late in summer, and as it grew, transplanted it into hanging baskets and into a round willow basket that stood on a bracket above my other plants. During the fall and winter, until February, I kept the shoots pinched back; it grew so rapidly that by spring it hung half a yard below the basket and was one sheet of beautiful blue. It remains in bloom for months. The more it is pinched back or picked, the more it blooms, and it sows itself in all the pots under it. As *they* grow, I transplant into baskets or boxes, for young plants are better than old ones."

The lobelia blossom is one of the loveliest true blues in the horticultural world, where many blues are nearer lavender. Lobelia, like alyssum, is another plant excellent for "clothing" a pot, planter, or window box planted with larger plants. Keep the lobelias well pinched, to promote shapeliness and persistent bloom. If you plan on using the flowers in an arrangement, pick them early and give them several hours to absorb water so they won't wilt. For a Fourth of July dinner one year we made tiny place markers with a red rose bud, white alyssum, and lobelia, the whole surrounded with geranium leaves.

Double-flowered geraniums such as this one were much prized by gardeners of the 19th century, who of course had no such spectacular varieties as today's free-flowering hybrids.

MIGNONETTE

Mignonette takes its name from the French for "the little darling." It is normally an annual, but if given winter protection it will grow, said old Peter Henderson, into a woody shrub known as tree mignonette and commonly thought of as a different species. If grown in too-rich soil, mignonette loses its fragrance—its most prized quality. To have mignonette in the house in winter, Henderson directed, sow seed in pots outdoors in July, thinning to no more than eight plants to the pot. About September bring the pots into a cool room to form flower buds. In October move them to the light in a room that "does not exceed 50° at night," where they will flower beautifully until March.

If your mignonette fails to sprout, the trouble may be ants, as a gardener told *Park's Floral Magazine* in 1879. She found the ants busily carrying off her seed, and promptly doused their hill with boiling water.

PANSIES

Pansies have been among the favorite annuals of gardeners for many years, being as willing to grow as they are lovely. Here is how a Harrisburg, Pennsylvania, gardener of the later 19th century handled her planting from one year to the next: "Year before last we sowed pansy seed about the first of May, in the ground, but put window glass a little raised over the spot and kept the ground always moist. They came up beautifully. When quite small we transplanted them six inches apart along the edge of a bed in a small shady back yard. From the first of August until the frosts came we had the finest pansies we ever saw outside a greenhouse. Late in the fall we prepared a very rough coldframe against the south side of the house, carefully lifted each plant and set them close together in this place. In February they began to bloom. Bouquets were cut every day, not one bloom was allowed to go to seed or wither on the stalk, and by this means they were kept in bloom until the first of May. The same stalks bloomed all summer in the open ground, having been cut back and set out in May. Self-sown seedlings almost as fine are now [the following spring] blooming in the coldframe."

Pansies are also popular with us, and one year we bordered a path through our vegetable garden with Swiss Giant pansies we had planted early, backing them with lemon thyme. The willingness of the pansy to please you was indicated in this item of December 27, 1877, from the Farmington (Maine) *Chronicle:* "Mrs. O.B. Butler gathered from her garden several perfectly developed pansies Friday, 21st inst. Pretty well for December, in Maine."

ROSES

In 1876 *The American Agriculturist* had this advice on growing this perennial indoors in winter: "Be sure that the roses have been *grown in pots*, and not taken up from the open ground and potted, as they rarely recover in time to be of much use. As to soil, it matters little what it is, provided it is porous, as liquid ma-

EIGHT EVERBLOOMING ROSES FOR 50 CTS.

These are not cheap roses, but choice varieties of strong growth and free-blooming habit, which have been carefully chosen and *grown in large quantities especially for this offer*. Being selected a year in advance we cannot make any changes in the collection and shall send the separate varieties at the prices given for each.

For 50 Cts. we shall send the entire collection of eight finest everblooming roses described below,—strong well-rooted plants, distinctly labeled, by mail, postpaid.

BURBANK. This grand rose, introduced by us, is the hardiest and most free-flowering rose for outdoor culture ever offered. It originated with MR. LUTHER BURBANK, to whom we paid $500.00 for the entire stock. The plant is of strong vigorous growth, with rich dark-green foliage, branching freely, of compact rounded bush habit, and wonderfully free flowering. A bed of this variety at FORDHOOK is in constant bloom from early in the summer until the flowers are cut off by severe freezing, without any protection whatever. Flowers are three inches in diameter, very double, and of a deep glowing rose-pink, shading to silvery rose in center. *See illustration.* 15 cts. each.

PAPA GONTIER. Strong vigorous growth, and producing large finely pointed buds of bright cherry-red; one of the best for pot-culture or for cut-flowers, and of the finest tea fragrance. 15 cts. each.

MOSELLA. This is similar in growth and flower to *Clotilde Soupert*, but differs in color, as the center of the flower is richly shaded with apricot-yellow. The flowers are not so double as those of Soupert, but make finer buds and more profuse bloom. 10 cts. each.

QUEEN'S SCARLET. Strong vigorous growth, with dark-green foliage. Flowers bright scarlet, shading lighter in the center. 10 cts. each.

KAISERIN AUGUSTA VICTORIA. The finest white rose for summer flowering; large pointed buds of purest snowy whiteness, strongly fragrant. 15 cts. each.

MAMAN COCHET. The best pink tea rose for summer bedding. The flowers are silvery rose, shaded with mauve and yellow. 10 cts.

CLOTILDE SOUPERT. Dwarf compact bush growth and profuse bloomer. Large and finely double flowers, pearly white with rose-pink center.

BRIDESMAID. Grand, large, finely formed buds of a deep rose-pink, produced freely on long stems. A popular favorite. 10 cts. each; 3 for 25 cts.

EIGHT RARE AND POPULAR ROSES FOR 60 CTS.

For 60 Cts. we shall mail one good strong plant of each variety of these **Eight Elegant Roses** described below. Separately, the varieties are sold at the prices quoted.

This collection offers an opportunity to our customers to secure the very finest new Roses at small expense.

LIBERTY. A grand new hybrid tea rose of strong vigorous growth, perfectly hardy, everblooming, and with the deep rich coloring of the *Jacqueminot*. The flowers are of large size, with thick heavy petals of a deep rich but very bright shade of crimson-red, having the substance and fragrance of the hardy June roses. For deep rich coloring it is the finest everblooming variety that has ever been introduced. 30 cts. each.

ROSETTE. Plant is of strong vigorous growth, with light-green foliage; a constant bloomer; the large and very double flowers are borne on long stems, being especially desirable as a cut-flower. The color is a rich deep pink, with lighter shade of rose bordering the velvety petals. A grand bedding or cemetery rose. 20 cts. each.

MRS. ROBERT GARRETT. A splendid variety, producing flowers of immense size; the buds are long and pointed; color a soft bright pink. 15 cts. each.

MADAME ABEL CHATENAY. Flowers of good size, full and double, of firm substance and delightfully fragrant. Color rosy carmine, blended with darker shadings. 15 cts. each.

PERLE DES JARDINS. An everblooming variety, having large, finely pointed buds. The opened flowers are large, very double, and full centered; color rich sulphur-yellow. 10 cts. each.

ETOILE DE LYON. This is the best yellow rose for bedding; of good growth and free flowering. Large, double, golden-yellow flowers. 10 cts. each.

WHITE MAMAN COCHET. Desirable for bedding. The best white everblooming variety. 15 cts. each. | **HERMOSA.** Flowers of good size, quite double, and of a soft rose-pink; very fragrant. 10 cts. each.

For One Dollar we shall mail both collections, the **Eight New Choice Everblooming Roses** and the **Eight Rare and Popular Roses, sixteen in all** of the very finest hardy everblooming varieties. With each order we shall send **our Booklet** giving directions for culture.

In 1901 the W. Atlee Burpee seed company was selling rose plants for a mere 10¢ to 30¢ each—and selling collections at cut rates such as eight for 60¢.

nure may be used if it is poor, but if it becomes soggy and close, the plants will fail. Roses when growing need at most a temperature of 70° in the daytime, and it may go fifteen or twenty degrees lower at night. Do not over-water; always let the soil get a little dry on the surface before watering. Turn the ball of earth out of the pot occasionally, and see if there are angle worms; if they cannot all be picked off, water with clear lime water. Shower as often as convenient; once a week at least, but twice or three times is better; set the pots in a bathtub or sink, and shower with a fine sprinkler. If plant lice [aphids] appear, shower with weak tobacco water. Sudden changes of temperature and cold drafts are apt to cause mildew, and should be avoided in airing. When a shoot has bloomed, cut it back to a good bud; do not be afraid to use the knife."

For those interested, this advice was offered in 1878: "The budding of roses should be attended to during the months of August and September. The buds should be inserted upon the north side of branches that have completed their growth for the season. A fine effect is produced by budding different kinds of roses upon the same stalk."

SWEET PEAS

Introduced into England from Sicily in 1701, according to Peter Henderson, the annual sweet pea became immensely popular in the United States in the 19th century, and new variety followed new variety. Its delightful fragrance has always endeared the flower to gardeners, together with its lovely and wide span of colors and its delicate texture of petal. In 1881 Henderson could say sweet peas "include white, purple, black, scarlet, blue-edged, and striped sorts," and seedsman W. Atlee Burpee, a foremost introducer of new varieties, could call them "the poor man's orchid."

In its 1897 catalog the Burpee company devoted its front cover and an entire 10-page section to sweet peas, more than the space given any single species, flower or vegetable. A featured

BURPEE'S SUMMER=FLOWERING BULBS.

The summer-flowering Bulbs for spring planting contained in the following list are *inexpensive, very easily grown,* and produce some of the most showy and beautiful of all summer and autumn flowers. There are but few flowers that can compare with the noble and brilliant spikes of the Gladiolus, the grace and elegance of the Lily, the purity and sweetness of the Tuberose, the majestic foliage of the Caladium, the flaming heads of the Tritoma, or the wonderful markings of the Tigridia. They require scarcely any care, and quickly make a gorgeous display, while the bulbs can be kept over winter, and will year after year continue to return a hundred-fold, in beauty and satisfaction, the trifling expense of the original cost. These bulbs are all grown for us in large quantities, true to name, and we have priced them very low to bring them within the reach of all. They are in splendid condition, fine, large bulbs, properly stored in our warehouse, and will be sent, securely packed, in the same parcels with flower or vegetable seeds. Our prices are for choice bulbs, **postpaid, by mail,** to any address in the United States.

NEW EXCELSIOR PEARL TUBEROSES.

The Tuberose is justly a universal favorite, and is very easily grown. It is the most popular of all flowers for button-hole bouquets during August and September. The **New Excelsior Pearl Tuberoses** have been selected with great care and are superior to the ordinary Pearl Tuberoses. This variety is characterized by its short, robust stem and long spikes of large flowers in great profusion, perfectly double and twice the size of the common Tuberose, while of equally delicious fragrance. We grow these bulbs in immense quantities for American and export trade, filling single orders for from 20,000 to 100,000 bulbs. We offer choice, large-flowering bulbs of this magnificent strain, by mail, at 6 for 20 cts.; 35 cts. per doz.; 25 for 70 cts.; 100 for $2.50, postpaid. Largest size selected bulbs, by mail, 5 cts. each; 6 for 25 cts.; 50 cts. per doz.; $3.00 per 100, postpaid. Or by express, at purchaser's expense: $2.00 per 100; 200 for $3.50, or $15.00 per 1000.

NEW BRANCHING ALBINO TUBEROSE.

A distinct new sort, sure to become popular. It flowers from twenty to thirty days earlier than the old single variety, and sends up two or more flower stems from the same bulb. The flower spike is large and evenly filled with large single flowers with gracefully recurved petals, free from the brown tint common to the old sorts. The tube and expanded sepals are of the purest waxy-white, and the odor is less heavy than in the older varieties. Altogether it is a most attractive plant for cut flowers. Although only of recent introduction, our large stock permits us to offer this valuable acquisition at a price within the reach of all.

Strong, blooming bulbs 10 cts. each; 3 for 25 cts.; 6 for 50 cts.; $1.00 per doz., by mail, postpaid,

VARIEGATED=LEAVED TUBEROSE.

The leaves of this variety are bordered with creamy-white; flowers single, but very large and of exquisite fragrance. Bulbs continue to grow and bloom year after year. It blooms several weeks earlier than the other sorts, which adds greatly to its value. 10 cts. each; 3 for 25 cts., or $1.00 per doz., by mail, postpaid.

ORANGE=FLOWERED TUBEROSE.

A very beautiful variety, with elegant single flowers. It is considered much hardier than any double Tuberose, and more certain to bloom early in the season. The exquisite pure snowy-white flowers rival orange blossoms in sweetness. We offer strong, blooming bulbs, 10 cts. each; 3 for 25 cts.; 6 for 50 cts.; $1.00 per doz.

"There are but few flowers," an old seed catalog stated, "that can compare with the purity and sweetness of the tuberose," and bulbs were offered at as little as 2½¢ each postpaid, if ordered in quantities.

item there was a tiny new kind, Cupid, that grew only five inches tall and bore white flowers. "The greatest novelty in flowers ever known," the seed house rashly announced to a breathless world— but a premature boast, it turned out, for Cupid was so very dwarf a plant, every passing shower splashed the little thing with mud, and it was soon regretfully withdrawn from the market in favor of splendid new taller varieties. As late as the 1930s the sweet pea was the most popular home garden annual flower in America, according to seed sales.

ARRANGING PLANTS
IN BEDS

This interesting if somewhat rigid advice appeared in the *Western Rural* magazine in 1879: "In arranging flowers in beds the principal things to be avoided are: The placing of rose-colored or red flowers next scarlet or orange, or orange next yellow, blue next violet, or rose next violet. On the contrary, the following colors harmonize: White will relieve any color, (but should not be placed next yellow), orange with light blue, yellow with violet, dark blue with orange-yellow, white with pink or rose, and lilac with yellow. By observing these rules, the amateur may have his flower borders vie in beauty and arrangement with those of greater pretensions and even surpass many of them."

Something called a tent bed was popular in the 19th century. "These are very ornamental," an old garden guide said. "They may be formed in a variety of ways, which good taste will suggest. The usual shape is round or oval, having a pole in the center and chains or ropes directed to the sides, to be covered with creepers—evergreen or annual, or both, on alternate wires."

In discussing the shapes to make flower beds, a floral magazine reader of 1877 suggested: "Take the leaf of an oak or a maple or any other leaf, the shape of which suits you, study its form, and then go to work and shape your bed like it, only larger.

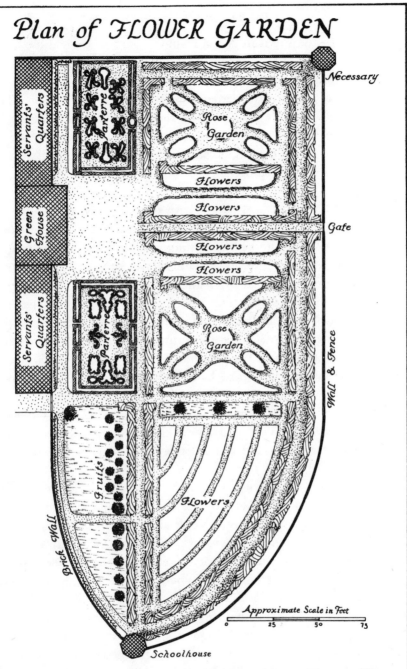

Plan of FLOWER GARDEN

Necessary

Servants' Quarters

Parterre

Rose Garden

Flowers

Flowers

Green House

Gate

Flowers

Flowers

Servants' Quarters

Parterre

Rose Garden

Wall & Fence

Brick Wall

Fruits

Flowers

Approximate Scale in Feet

0   25   50   75

Schoolhouse

The flower garden of George Washington's Mount Vernon, like
its companion the kitchen garden, flanked a bowling green designed by Washington. The domestic records do not say what
flowers were in the garden in his day, but shrubs and fruit trees
were included, and like the kitchen garden, the flower garden's
design had a striking resemblance to that of English country-
house gardens of the time.

Another easy way is to take a map of some country and use it for a copy, making walks for the principal rivers, low blue flowers for lakes, and high purple ones for mountains, red for cities, &c.''

We found this approach interesting for this reason: The landscape architect who planned the Luther Burbank memorial garden in Santa Rosa, California, arrived at the design by studying those of split seeds, a procedure of which Burbank would have thoroughly approved.

CUTTINGS

An old way to start cuttings (or to germinate seed) was to prepare a miniature hotbed by putting a layer of fresh manure in a shallow box and covering it with a layer of mixed earth, sand, and powdered charcoal. After this had stood for a few days it was watered lightly, the cuttings were pushed into it, and a pane of glass was laid on top. The bottom heat from the manure helped the cuttings to root. You can substitute warm, half-finished compost for the manure. We get bottom heat by setting pots, cans, or flats of cuttings on top of half-finished compost in the compost bin.

This suggestion was passed along in 1879: ''In Germany pulverized charcoal is used for striking [rooting] cuttings, and is found better than sand as it supplies nourishment after they are rooted.''

Some 19th-century gardeners wrapped the lower ends of their cuttings with damp moss for one or more days before inserting in the rooting mixture. ''Never allow cuttings to become wilted before insertion,'' the gardener was warned, ''and always allow several leaves to remain on each to elaborate the sap and assist in forming roots. Do not crowd your cuttings, as this will often cause them to damp off.''

In the 1880s a lady in Texas wrote fellow gardeners: ''I plant the cutting in ready-made soil, turn a glass over it, let it alone except to keep it damp. When new shoots appear, take the glass off, keep in the shade until strong, then put it where it belongs. I rarely fail. I raise hundreds for friends."

Many times we have kept a deck or patio colorful all summer with potted plants grown from cuttings. At the end of the season we moved the plants to the garden if the climate permitted, and had more young pot plants from slips coming along for next season. This is a particularly good plan with an expensive large-flowered petunia. In this way, for no expense, you can renew window box plants and those in pots and planters. The important thing in growing such plants as Cecile Brunner roses, nasturtiums, and fuchsias in pots is to pinch back some of the new growth regularly. This keeps them shapely and free-flowering. And so treated, they need no supports.

FROST PROTECTION   Evergreen branches were a favored mulch for protection of plants from cold, and in the 1880s an Oregon rose grower wrote *Park's Floral Magazine* that his hybrid tea La France had survived seven degrees below zero with this protection. "You can set me down as strongly in favor of evergreen boughs as the surest and safest way of protecting roses," he wrote. "One more advantage which they have is that they can remain on during a warm spell and do no hurt, which is not true of leaves, manure, and cloth, which are liable to heat."

In contrast, a very new protection for roses from cold weather is a liquid plastic spray following a dormant-spray coating. Both sprays are available at garden suppliers. The plastic one is to hold moisture in the plant tissues during dormancy. Our own inclination is toward the evergreen protection, although we admit this is from a preference to near-to-nature gardening.

GARDEN ETIQUETTE

For polite behavior in the flower garden of a friend in the middle Victorian years, we give you this guidance from the *Farmers' Advocate:*

"If the walks are narrow, a little care will avoid sweeping one's skirts over the beds to the injury of the flowers and the nerves of the owner as well. Do not pick unbidden a blossom, or even a leaf—it may be the very one its possessor values the most.

"Nothing is more presumptuous than to return from a ramble in a friend's garden with a bouquet of your own selection, unless requested in an unequivocal manner to help yourself.

"The beauty of scented-leaved plants is often ruined from having their foliage pinched by odor-loving friends."

GARDENLESS GARDEN

Under the heading "Ornamenting a Verandah," this advice from an 1879 gardener may be of interest today to someone considering how to plant for privacy on a patio, a condominium balcony, or some other such summery hideaway:

"A friend has a small yard and a large dog, two possessions incompatible with a great floral display. Her house has a verandah fronting upon the street, and she determined to make that the base of operations. She had wooden boxes made of lengths to fit between the posts and painted to match the house. They were a foot wide and about as deep, perforated with holes through the bottom and set on thick boards so that water was conducted over the edge of the porch, to drip on the ground.

"Then she had the boxes filled with rich soil, setting out plants which would give a good display for the summer, making scarlet and white the prevailing tints. At the posts she set out vines which were trained upon them, and in the front of the boxes sweet alyssum made a mass of white drooping over. The effect was extremely pretty, and a screen behind which the family could sit with a greater feeling of retirement."

HANGING BASKETS

This suggestion for a "Novel Hanging Basket" appeared in an old gardening magazine; we suggest using a chunky Oxheart carrot.

"Take a nice, large, good-shaped carrot, cut off about a third of the part that grows in the ground, scrape out the inside until only a shell is left, fill it with earth, put in cypress vine, thunbergia, or morning glory seeds (or all if you like), suspend the carrot by cords in a sunny window, keep the earth quite wet, and you will soon have a pretty variety. The carrot itself will sprout from top, or rather the bottom as it is upside down, and the foliage of that is quite pretty."

An advantage of the carrot basket is, it will not drip. To get around that fault of most other hanging baskets, a gardener of several generations ago suggested her own device: "In the center of a moss-lined basket I place a small goblet, leaving only an inch or two above the surface. In this I anchor by means of a small weight a dozen or more strands of loosely twisted worsted of varying lengths, some hanging over the edge of the glass, others reaching to the outer edge of the basket. Then, filling the goblet with water I leave the basket to water itself at its leisure. Two days is sufficient to empty the reservoir; the earth is kept constantly moist, and no water drips on the floor." This wick method of watering has been used in recent times to water plants while the owner is on vacation.

183

HOUSE PLANTS

Here is Henry Ward Beecher's advice to the ladies of the mid-19th century on caring for what he called parlor flowers:

"Water freely such as are in pots, while in blossom. The flower stalks will be apt to shoot up taller and weaker than in the garden, and will require rods to support them. Let the rod be thrust down about two inches from the centre of the flower, and attach the flower stem to it by one or two ligaments. Flowers in small stove rooms can be kept in health with extreme difficulty. The heat forces their growth, or injures the leaves. They should be washed off once a week, as the dust settles on the leaf and stops up the stomata (mouths) by which the leaf perspires and breathes. If green aphides infest them, put a pan of coals beneath the stand and throw on a half-handful of coarse tobacco. In half an hour every insect will tumble off. Let such as lie on the surface of the earth be removed or crushed, as they will else revive. Plants should have fresh air every day."

To a lady who complained her plants had no flowers in winter, old seedsman George Park advised she seed Chinese primroses and cinerarias, and plant bulbs of Roman hyacinth, paper white narcissus, and jonquils.

Experimenting with water temperatures for house plants, a French writer in 1886 found cold water best, especially for Chinese primroses. Another gardener of the period noted: "English ivy seems to like cold water."

Remarking that over-watering was the most common cause of sickly house plants, a gardener of 1879 gave her treatment of such a plant: "Cease to give it anything, and let the soil become dry or nearly so, when the plant should be removed from the pot and the soil gently crushed between the hands just enough to loosen the outer crust so that it will shake off." She then repotted it in fresh soil in a clean pot.

This sound watering advice came from the Worcester, Massachusetts, *Gazette* a century ago: "With experience one can soon tell by the weight of the pot. When very wet the weight is nearly double. The color of the earth will also tell when it needs water. It is almost always much lighter in color when dry. The feel of the earth will soon teach one to know when a plant needs water. When dry, the earth will crumble a little when touched. Plants will need more water in a warm room; in a dry atmosphere; when growing vigorously; when in good health; and when in light sandy earth."

In the 19th century, as today, opinions differed on whether to turn house plants. An Ohio gardener stated: "I think it best to turn window plants, for the beauty goes to the light, and when turned they look so fresh and green and cheerful." But said an Illinois gardener: "I never turn my plants in winter. If a plant is turned often it will not bloom well." Another gardener said she turned hers every day or two," "but during the short days of December and January I do not turn the flower buds away from the light till well developed."

185

A simple night winter protection for house plants near a window is this old one: "Don't forget to pin a newspaper around your choicest plants these cold nights. A five-cent newspaper will keep out more frost than a five-dollar blanket."

At one time the eggplant was grown for ornament as a pot plant. "They are curious and interesting," said a gardening dictionary of the 1870s. "The scarlet variety is a great novelty." If you are intrigued, a good choice for a potted eggplant would be one of the small-fruited ones.

PERENNIALS

Here is some advice on ornamental perennials from a gardeners' publication of a century ago: "Perennials are those sorts or classes of flowers which, once planted, grow on from year to year and can be readily increased by division of roots. Nearly all varieties may be increased by seed. Many bloom the first year from seed if sown early. Seed may be sown early in spring where strong plants are wanted the first season, or in early summer to produce a stock of plants for the following summer. They may be taken up every year thereafter and the roots divided and reset."

A good way to get such plants is to just let it be known you want some. Most gardeners cannot bear to throw away surplus plants. A friend in Missouri was a scandal to her friends for the money she spent on new iris hybrids. But by their third season the new was old-hat and our own iris beds reaped the harvest. In another locality we made the acquaintance of a basset hound who one day turned up with owner in tow bearing a huge box of Shasta daisy plants just thinned from a bed. And a generous gardener in Carmel, California, every now and then puts a cardboard box in front of her cottage, heaped with surplus plants, and with a sign: "These are _____. Help yourself."

PLANTERS

Victorian-Age flower gardeners contrived fanciful ways to show off their prides and joys, such as monumental stands—one of which was topped with an old stove firebox. Here is one lady's notion: "Take an old-fashioned night stand and nail a box about a foot square on the top. Take cement and border the table with pebbles of curious form and color. Then arrange shells, nice cones, and stones tastefully and carelessly between the border and the box. Fill the box with rich soil, and plant myrtle, tradescantia, German ivy, and other trailing vines around the edge, and put a vase containing a hyacinth bulb in the center. The vines will reach the floor in a short time, and present a lovely appearance."

Then there was the so-called "stump mania." A 19th-century gardener related how a young friend "went hunting a hollow stump through the woods and found one hollow to the very bottom, and begged it of the owner. The father cut the roots off good length, took it home, turned it upside down, setting it well into the earth, filled it with soil for her, and then she set it with various colored, hardy sedums properly arranged, hung tiny baskets with vines on the projecting roots (after tacking wood mosses all over them), and it's just beautiful and curious to look at."

Another gardener made what she named a chair stand: "On an old chair with the back off I nailed a washtub, in the center of which I fastened an upright post four feet long, having four arms projecting within about a foot of the top. On the top of the post I nailed a board on which I placed a pot of oxalis. The projecting arms supported hanging baskets, while the tub was filled with earth in which were climbing and drooping plants, the former in the center and the latter around the margin, the intervening space being taken up with a profuse blooming little plant bearing bright colored flowers. A Maderia vine enveloped the upright post with a mass of verdure and flowers, and the whole thing was a thing of beauty and much admired by all."

POTTING

Potting is a subject that has concerned gardeners for centuries. This advice was offered a hundred years ago: "A plant should not be potted when it is very dry nor when soaked. In the former case it is likely to remain dry, as water will pass through the fresh soil without penetrating the old ball of earth." An experienced nurseryman of the same era gave this transplanting tip: "I plunge the roots into water, then pour over them fine street dust; this gives all the little roots a coating of soil with which to begin."

To get potting soil, another gardener advised, "Cut a lot of good stiff sods as early in the season as possible. Let them be thrown into a heap and dug over two or three times during the summer. If the sods are dug from clay land, add a little sand. This, when it is broken fine, makes the best potting soil that I ever tried." Gardeners will recognize the procedure as a form of composting.

Here is Henry Ward Beecher's word on digging a plant for potting: "Select the pot, draw a circle around the plant the size of the pot, then thrust a sharp spade down so as to cut all the roots at the line of the circle. Let the plant remain, watering it thoroughly, and if it droops, let it be sheltered from the sun. In a few days new roots will begin to form, and in three or four weeks it may be carefully lifted, placed in the pot, and it will go on growing as if nothing had happened to it."

Foliage plants, said an old hand of 1878, needed large pots and rich soil, "but for such plants as are wanted to furnish flowers in abundance, small pots should be used. Of these we might mention fuchsias, geraniums, cupheas, begonias or flowering strains, abutilons, and others."

TUSSIE-MUSSIES

That charming conceit, the tussie-mussie, is still as appreciated today as in colonial times. Its construction is precise, a central flower surrounded by smaller ones. For instance, a large rosebud is encircled with white alyssum, then there may be a circle of forget-me-nots, one of tiny pink rosebuds, another of lavender ageratum, and finally a circle of mignonette for fragrance. The stems of all are passed through an X-slit in a lacepaper doily, a rubber band holds the doily around the stems and the stems are wrapped with foil.

We make tussies with whatever the garden offers at the time. Several hours beforehand we gather the flowers and put them in water at once; it is best to do so right in the garden as you gather them, then keep them in a cool dark place until ready for arranging. Have facial tissue or paper napkins, depending on the size of the tussie to be made, folded in three or four thicknesses and in widths suited to the length of the stems. Starting with the central flower held in the left hand, arrange the first circle around it and just slightly lower; then wrap tissue or napkin three or four times around the stems. Repeat this procedure with each of the other flower circles. Then surround the whole with rather stiff leaves such as those of Martha Washington geraniums or camellia. At this point, if the tussie is not to be presented immediately, we immerse the stems in a glass of water. When ready to complete the little thing we dry the stems with a towel, wrap another layer of paper around them, slip the doily on, and mold a piece of foil around the stems right up to the leaves and flowers. If you have hardened the flowers well, the arrangement will last for hours, even when carried in a warm hand—which is what a tussie-mussie is for.

We have made them from tiny four-inch-wide ones, on up to glamorous foot-wide kinds in a spectrum of color and form. For a festival queen and court we harmonized flower colors with gowns and added streamers of inch-wide ribbon with love knots holding tiny flowers represented in the bouquets. Two of the most appreciated ones were made of only Martha Washington geraniums because they were all that the garden had in perfection at the time. We selected two colors, one for each tussie, for two small girls who were assistant hostesses at their artist-grandmother's one-woman show.

For real fun, try a vegetable tussie. Start with a fine fresh and plump radish with its little tail root left on. Hold it upside down and surround it with curled parsley. Follow with a circle of tiny carrots, then with a circle of a herb—thyme, basil, or marjoram—and frame the whole with nasturtium leaves. There—a delicious, old-fashioned bouquet.

WARDIAN CASES

Directions for setting up a tiny indoor garden in a Wardian case, the original terrarium, or "parlour greenhouse" as it was called soon after its invention in the mid-19th century, were given by the New York *Weekly Herald* as the winter of 1877-78 approached. A Wardian case looked like a box-shaped aquarium, and one can be substituted for it. Get a sheet of glass for a lid, and proceed according to the *Weekly Herald*'s directions:

> Lay bits of charcoal in the bottom to the depth of an inch and cover with eight inches of soil—of peat, sand, and leafmold in equal parts well mixed but not sifted. For plants, ferns, mosses, and early spring flowers from our woods will answer admirably. In the earth clinging to the roots of ferns will be seeds and roots of wild flowers which will grow and bloom in your Wardian case. It will be a constant source of happy surprise to watch the starting of new plants and the unrolling of each tiny frond of the ferns. Many meadow and swamp plants will also thrive well.
>
> Cut off damaged or dead foliage, and place plants firmly in the soil but do not crowd them. Give a slight watering and shade the case for a few days.
>
> Leaving the case open for a couple of hours each day will give ventilation. Keep soil moist but not sodden. Gentle sunlight is beneficial. Keep the case closed when the sun is on it.

In the fall of 1877 the Farmington, Maine, *Chronicle*, carried a story we think worth ending on as a final glorious example of floral appreciation a century ago, anticlimax notwithstanding.

The event recounted here took place in a small town, Temple, near Farmington.

> Three years ago Mrs. Henry Conant sent to Washington and procured the rare plant, a night-blooming cereus. About sunset last Wednesday she saw indications of the approaching event for which she had so eagerly looked, and being generous as well as somewhat of an enthusiast in floriculture, she sent out and invited in her neighbors to enjoy with herself the rare sight.
>
> By 10 o'clock a large number of people had gathered at the house, no one of whom had ever before witnessed the phenomenon. Before midnight the flower had completely unfolded, presenting one of the most beautiful floral exhibitions we ever beheld. The flower when in full bloom measured thirteen inches in diameter. The enjoyment of the occasion was not a little heightened by enlivening music in which a large number participated, and at about midnight the company dispersed, feeling that they had been compensated for being called, as some of them were, from their beds, and for the discomfort of a drenching rain in which they returned to their homes.

CHAPTER

NINE

What's Ahead for the Home Gardener

UP TO now we have been looking backward, seeing what gardeners were doing during the past two centuries that we can put to good use today. Now we are going to give you a look ahead at gardening during the rest of the 20th century.

To do so, we asked some questions of a panel of experts in various fields—the Secretary of Agriculture, the heads of two national garden club organizations, a spokesman for environmentalists, gardening magazine editors, and some leading suppliers of seeds and plants. Here is what we asked them, and their answers.

Since the Secretary of Agriculture of the United States is there to help all citizens who grow food, we addressed this question to Secretary Earl L. Butz: "What can home gardeners best do to supplement commercial vegetable supplies during the next several years?" Mr. Butz's answer recommends an intensive use of space, from acreage to pots. He says:

192

It is evident that home vegetable gardening is once again becoming more popular and a greater part of the life-style of many citizens.

As more people settled in urban areas in the 20th century, these city dwellers increasingly gave up home and community gardening. That trend now seems to be reversing. With the interest in ecology and the necessity to conserve energy and cope with the cost of living, more people are beginning to grow their own fruits and vegetables. In view of that, we should provide our would-be gardeners with the know-how to be successful.

Most everyone can find a way to garden if he wants to —whether it is children gardening in a school yard, or apartment dwellers with a few pots on the balcony, or back-yard gardeners, or people sharing a community garden.

Vegetable gardening is a useful, enjoyable activity. It provides recreation, education, conservation, and the joy of eating one's own fresh vegetables.

Mrs. Howard S. Kittel, president of the large 50-year-old National Council of State Garden Clubs, was asked to venture a prediction as to the activity of home vegetable gardeners during the next two decades or so, and she characterized it with the interesting term: "Creative gardening." Here is how she justifies the description:

We see tomorrow's home gardeners as developers of completely new varieties of vegetables. Through horticultural knowledge, ingenuity, and singleness of purpose, we believe desirable food crops unavailable from commercial sources will be developed.

In addition we foresee increasingly healthy soil and stronger, more disease-resistant plants which will keep producing in spite of unfavorable weather conditions—and insects. Natural aids such as biological controls, plant-based sprays, companion planting, etc., will continue to evolve as individual experimentation expands.

As gardeners of the future become increasingly knowledgeable, we believe chemical gardening practices will be phased out and simpler, more natural techniques developed.

A mellow air of nostalgia came through in the response to the question of what the next 25 years will be like in home gardening, from Harold J. Parnham, president of the Men's Garden Clubs of America:

Dinner at Grandma's always seemed to taste better. And it really did. Grandma had a garden. With the large majority of people now living in smaller homes or even apartments in the urban areas, and with more time on our hands, and higher prices, and, it appears, with less gas to run around and do nothing, I feel that there will be more home vegetable growing.

Small plots at apartment sites are becoming very popular. In crowded space, people will find they can grow vegetables among flowers, edging flower beds with small vegetables and growing vining types up trellises and poles above limited areas. Newer varieties will produce more, and second and third plantings will be practical. AND they will taste just like Grandma's did.

Mr. Parnham concluded with this eye-to-the-future item: "The Men's Garden Clubs are placing great stress on Youth Gardening, and it's taking hold."

For a look at future home gardening vis-a-vis the overall ecological scene, we asked for a reaction from Justin Blackwelder, president of The Environmental Fund, headquartered in Washington, D.C. "Home gardening," Mr. Blackwelder comments, "will not solve the food/population problem. But," he then adds, "it may help a great deal to balance some household budgets, and it will certainly improve American diets. In addition, millions of people are going to wonder why they lived so long without ever tasting truly fresh vegetables—most vegetables being rather dismal affairs even a day or two after they are harvested."

The next group of knowledgeable people we sought opinions from consisted of gardening-magazine editors. Our question to them was: "What should home gardeners stress to best help in the national food situation during the next two decades?" Each reply was specific, and each was quite different from the others.

Miss Rachel Snyder, editor-in-chief of *Flower and Garden Magazine* as well as a botanist and author, recommends that gardeners be open-minded and experimental, "and then crow about their successes. At basis of this suggestion is the conviction that many a worthy vegetable lies as yet undiscovered by most home gardeners. Because of ignorance, we are all deprived of many a tasty and nutritious vegetable we might be enjoying if only we knew about it."

As to why this is so, Miss Snyder suggests: "We are too hemmed in by our traditions on food. In America we have been too stuck on carry-overs from cool European climates that do not do well over large areas of this country. I anticipate that we may learn many useful things from China in years to come."

Robert Rodale is the son of the late J.I. Rodale, who founded *Organic Gardening and Farming* magazine, a pilot publication in advocating gardening without factory-made pest controls and fertilizers. Robert Rodale is now editor and publisher of the magazine, and his response to our question put particular stress on a gardening possibility open to anyone, even citizens with not a square inch of garden space. He says:

> I think that gardeners can best help the national food situation in the next two decades by learning how to make 'earth sprouts.' These are edible sprouts of seeds like mung beans, soybeans, and various grains and pulses that are

grown in soil rather than being sprouted in water, as is customary. Young tender sprouts contain a much higher percentage of vitamins than the seeds from which they grow. And sprouts that are made in contact with earth contain more vitamins than water sprouts. Using this method, therefore, will multiply the supply of food available to people, at no extra cost in energy.

I think it will provide a very convenient source of badly needed fresh vegetables and salad ingredients for people at all times of the year, regardless of whether they live on the land or are living in an apartment. This is perhaps the best aspect of this method.

Organic Gardening and Farming instructed its readers to grow earth sprouts by pre-soaking 4 ounces of seeds for 12 hours, then scattering them evenly over a 3″ layer of soil in a box about a foot square and nearly as high. A light covering of soil is added, the box is covered with a lid, and in four days with no further attention about 2 pounds of sprouts are ready for washing and eating. The method takes much less attention than the usual water-sprouting.

Space-finding was also prominent in the response from Edwin F. Steffek, author, and editor of the prestigious national magazine *Horticulture*, published by the Massachusetts Horticultural Society. "I strongly suggest," Mr. Steffek says, "that home gardeners investigate fully the possibilities of combining edible crops with their ornamentals. In many ways a good looking vegetable is just as ornamental as a flower. By edible crops I mean to include bush and tree fruits of all kinds as well as vegetables. If necessary, gardeners should concentrate upon space-saving dwarfs. Further, if space permits, I strongly suggest their giving serious thought to the nut crops and the less common fruits as well. At the same time, I do not suggest that they curtail their ornamental gardening.

"Fertilizer should be used with care and thought, so the maximum results are obtained with the minimum amounts."

Next, we turned to suppliers of seeds and plants, those indispensable people whose eyes are always focused on the future—to the new things we'll be planting three, five, ten years from now. The seedsmen here serve, among them, all parts of the country. Their answers were made in response to our question: "What new trends do you see coming in home vegetable gardening in the next 10 to 25 years?"

They name a total of twelve such trends and are unanimous on two of them: *higher quality* vegetables and more *compact* plants. Interestingly, both these points are in large measure responsible for the popularity of new midget vegetables in recent years. There is near-unanimity on two other trends: varieties that are more *disease-resistant*, and that are more *productive*. Here are the seedsmen and the other points they made.

David Burpee, whose father established the internationally big W. Atlee Burpee Company in 1876, predicts "many new varieties and hybrids, many of them earlier maturing." Earliness is welcome to anyone but in addition is a highly important quality for gardeners whose growing seasons are short, sometimes making the difference between being able or not at all able to grow a particular crop.

Mr. Burpee further predicts: "There will also be more compact and more productive varieties of hybrids." Modern hybrid vegetables, it should be noted, have the vigor that also came with old-time hybrid ones, but the new ones are also consistent performers—which the old ones were not.

Mr. Burpee also expects to see new vegetables with wider climatic adaptibility, "including cantaloupes," he notes, such as a new crenshaw already on the market, "that will be grown farther north than ever before," and also bush types. In addition, he anticipates the other ordinarily vining plants, cucumbers and watermelons, growing on little bushes instead of vines. This is already true of some squashes.

197

William J. Park, president of his family's long-established southern house, Geo. W. Park Seed Company, sees the growing interest in home gardening bringing about the development of vegetables with a longer harvest period, "rather than ripening in a short season—which is, of course, what commercial growers want."

In addition, Mr. Park takes a look at seed costs, an increasingly significant gardening expense. He sees them rising, for two cogent reasons: "Greater research; but primarily the competition for cropland. The farmers who grow our seed crops will of course produce those which are the most profitable for them. Therefore the home gardener's vegetables compete with the major crops of the world, such as wheat, soybeans, and corn." It is a point worth close attention from all home gardeners, and recommends prudent use of seeds, and proper storage between seasons (as detailed in Chapter 6).

Kenneth E. Relyea, president of the well-known Farmer Seed & Nursery Company of Fairibault, Minnesota, makes a point that has particular significance for home gardeners: "In the future . . . we will see varieties that are bred and researched strictly as home-garden varieties and not, as has been in the past, researched and developed mainly for the processor and then spun off to the home gardener if he wanted to use them."

Mr. Relyea continues: "I think also that you will see an increase in the number of bacterial insecticides like Thuricide in the future. It seems to be a very logical way to control undesirable insects on a specific basis."

This thought was also expressed by Charles B. Wilson of the highly respected Joseph Harris Company, Rochester, New York: "A great deal of research is being done on biological insect control such as the microbial insecticides which attack only the insects they are designed to kill and have no effect on any other creatures. . . . In the future a wide range of biological insecticides of many different types will be available." And to this prediction Mr. Wilson added one that has been the secret dream of all gardeners ever since gardening began: "Plants with resistance to insect damage are not yet available, but they are coming. For example, it will not be long before we can grow sweet corn with husks tough enough to resist corn borers and earworms."

Mr. Wilson believes that the recent boom in home vegetable gardening will outlive the "economic conditions that triggered it," and draws this long-term conclusion: "This will mean that the efforts to develop vegetables of ever-higher quality will be more strongly emphasized than ever. With little relief in sight for world-wide food shortages, much research is being devoted to crops with higher nutritional value, and in time, the home gardener will benefit from these developments."

We asked Paul Stark, Jr., to speak on behalf of the nation's nurserymen supplying home gardeners with fruit trees. An internationally-known pomologist, Mr. Stark is vice president and research head of the oldest U.S. nursery, Stark Bro's, of Louisiana, Missouri.

Overall, he looks to variety improvements as accounting for the big gains he sees coming for home gardeners. These gains may be summarized as higher-quality fruits, earlier ripening and later ripening varieties, an extension of growing areas both northward and southward, more disease-resistant trees, and more fruit per foot of garden space. Here, in Mr. Stark's words, are some of the specifics:

"Much emphasis will be placed on developing better varieties for the early and late parts of the growing season. Some of these are coming on the scene now, like the Jerseymac apple from Rutgers that gives us a good McIntosh apple a month earlier. The new selection is also adapted to more southern growing regions where regular McIntosh does not perform too well due to long hot summers. New and better varieties of peaches and nectarines are being introduced for the very early season right after cherries and apricots are harvested." Mr. Stark then adds this extremely important point: "These will be easier to grow, as earlier ripening will simplify insect and disease control."

In sweet cherries, a new one from Canada, Stella, needs no cross-pollinator to set fruit, an excellent trait since "many yards have room for only one sweet cherry tree. . . . Stella also sets well in bad weather during the bloom season."

Peach and nectarine growing, says Mr. Stark, is being extended farther north by the development of "hardiness against low winter temperatures and spring freezes," Reliance and Monroe being two varieties with such characteristics. And peach growing is being extended southward into Florida, Texas, and southern California with the development of new varieties such as Desert Gold, that can break dormancy with fewer hours of winter chilling, "where only 300 to 500 hours of below-45° F. are experienced." This is also the case with some varieties of apples, Mr. Stark says, such as Beverly Hills and the recently introduced Tropical Beauty.

And the highly important trend toward built-in disease resistance continues: "Prima and Priscilla apples are already available with good scab or black rot resistance." Scab, mildew, and rust are practically unknown, Mr. Stark adds, with another new apple, Surprize, a Golden Delicious type, and he sees virus-free trees for all major fruits in the future, a research achievement not much known to most home fruit gardeners but of great importance for healthier trees.

And for gardeners with space only for small fruits, Mr. Stark has this final good news: "New red raspberries such as Southland adapt this fine fruit to warm-summer zones. A good mulching program has also helped increase production and quality." And for your future planning: "Bigger and better strawberries that bear more are being developed, some yielding fruit all summer and into the fall."

Finally, to all the intriguing forecasts of gardening-to-come and new things already here, we would add one bit of urging, always good but sometimes mislaid. It is: Enjoy your garden. Visit it often—in early morning, not only perhaps to surprise some invading insect, but to see the shimmering dew on leaf and petal, to find a robin already engrossed with his day's business. Drop in on your garden at high noon, with the din of bees pleasantly in your ears, when herb and flower fragrances are sweetest. At dusk you'll find your plants glorying in the evening cool after a warm day. And by moonlight or starlight a garden possesses a dreamlike quiet, nature's own tranquilizer.

Never let a garden become a common scold, constantly nagging, giving no satisfaction of a job well done. It should be a joyous place, offering new delights each day—tiny seedlings just pushing above ground, the first rosy radish to be eaten at once, the rush of the late summer harvest, the exultation of getting everything snatched in on the heels of the first fall frost, and the thrill of going into a snowy landscape and bringing back to the warm kitchen your own carrots, parsnips, or salsify for a winter meal. Possess your garden and cherish it all through the seasons. That's what a garden is for.

Appendix

BURGESS SEED AND PLANT COMPANY, Galesburg, Michigan
49053

W. ATLEE BURPEE COMPANY, Warminster, Pennsylvania 18974;
Clinton, Iowa 52732; Riverside, California 92502

DE GIORGI COMPANY, Council Bluffs, Iowa 51501

FARMER SEED AND NURSERY COMPANY, Faribault, Minnesota
55021

HENRY FIELD SEED AND NURSERY COMPANY, Shenandoah, Iowa
51602

GURNEY SEED AND NURSERY COMPANY, Yankton, South Dakota
57078

JOSEPH HARRIS COMPANY, 3670 Buffalo Road, Rochester, New
York 14624

HEMLOCK HILL HERB FARM, Litchfield, Connecticut 06759

JOHNNY'S SELECTED SEEDS, N. Dixmont, Maine 04932

KITAZAWA SEED COMPANY, 356 W. Taylor Street, San Jose, California 95110

LE JARDIN DU GOURMET, W. Danville, Vermont 05873

J. E. MILLER NURSERIES, Canandaigua, New York 14424

NEW YORK STATE FRUIT TESTING CO-OPERATIVE ASSOCIATION, Geneva, New York 14456

NICHOLS GARDEN NURSERY, 1190 N. Pacific Highway, Albany, Oregon 97321

L. L. OLDS SEED COMPANY, P.O. Box 1069, Madison, Wisconsin 53701

GEORGE W. PARK SEED COMPANY, Greenwood, South Carolina 29647

R. H. SHUMWAY SEEDSMAN, P.O. Box 777, Rockford, Illinois 61101

SOUTHMEADOW FRUIT GARDENS, 2363 Tilbury Place, Birmingham, Michigan 48009

STOKES SEEDS, Box 548, Main Post Office, Buffalo, New York 14240

THOMPSON & MORGAN, 401 Kennedy Boulevard, Somerdale, New Jersey 08083

GARDENING MAGAZINES

THE AVANT GARDENER, P.O. Box 489, New York, N.Y. 10028. Published twice monthly, this newsletter-type publication provides a running commentary on the latest things in horticulture; especially useful to the serious hobby-gardener.

FLOWER AND GARDEN MAGAZINE, 4251 Pennsylvania Avenue, Kansas City, Missouri 64111. This well-respected monthly magazine covers the nation in three regional editions and takes up all aspects of home gardening.

HORTICULTURE, 300 Massachusetts Avenue, Boston, Massachusetts 02115. The Massachusetts Horticultural Society is publisher of this handsome monthly magazine. Coverage is national, and articles are by recognized experts; experienced gardeners comprise much of the audience.

ORGANIC GARDENING AND FARMING, Organic Park, Emmaus, Pennsylvania 18049. A lively monthly magazine, pocket-sized and packed with a wide variety of gardening and love-of-the-land articles. Readers contribute many personal experience items; staff articles are frequently in-depth studies. Coverage is national, and the entire emphasis is keyed to gardening in harmony with nature.

Index

abrasives, plants used as, 140
after-planting. *See* Transplanting
alecost. *See* Costmary
alum, as pesticide, 44
alyssum, 168-69
amaryllis, miticide for, 44
ammonia, as fertilizer, 20
anise:
 as flavoring, 112; as tea, 142; *See also* Florence fennel
ants, 32, 34, 173
aphids, 34-35
apple trees:
 new varieties of, 199-200; webworm pesticide for, 36-37
apricot water, 143
artichoke:
 globe, 54, 155; Jerusalem, 80-81
ashes:
 as cucumber beetle pesticide, 51; as fertilizer, 20-21; as slug repellent, 50
asparagus, 55
 winter storage of, 126
asparagus chicory, 56
azaleas, 24

balm, 113
 as flavoring, 113; medical use of, 156; as tea, 142
balsam, 169
balsam apple, medical use of, 157
bark insects and pests, 35
basil, 113
 as flavoring, 113; vinegar, 165; winter storage of, 130
Batavian endive, 77
beans, 56-57
 broad, 56-57; castor, 22, 47-48, 155; common, 56; English, 56-57; Fava, 57; fertilizer for, 20; kidney, 56; lima, 56; planting with corn, 57; snap, 56; soy, 57; winter storage of, 126-27
bee balm, as tea, 142
Beecher, Henry Ward:
 on cutworm control, 39; on house plants, 184-85
 Plain and Pleasant Talk about;

Fruits, Flowers and Farming, 2
 on planting potatoes, 9; on potting, 188; vegetable garden of, 54; on weeding, 18
beets, 57-58
 rotation of, 11; as rouge, 148; winter storae of, 127
Belgian endive. *See* Chicory
beverages, plants used as, 140-43;
 coffees, 140-41; dandelion wine, 142; teas, 142-43; waters, 143
Bible leaf, *See* Costmary
birds, as pests, 35-36
blackberry water, 143
Blackwelder, Justin, 194-95
blood meal, 104
blue aphids, 35
bones:
 as clubroot preventive, 38; to control ants, 34; as fertilizer, 21
bonnets, plants used as, 144
borage, 113-14
 flower candy, 144
brassicas, flea beetle pesticide for, 40
broccoli, 58
broom corn, 145
Brussels sprouts, 59
 winter storage of, 127
Burbank, Luther, 180
burdock, 59-60
burned earth, as fertilizer, 21-22
burnet, 60
 as flavoring, 114
Burpee, David, 197
butter leaves. *See* Orach
Butz, Earl L., 192-93

cabbages, 60-61
 clubroot in, 38; cutworm control in, 38, 39; fertilizer for, 20; maggot control in, 41; rotation of, 10, 38; winter storage of, 127
calendula, 114
 as flavoring, 114; medical use of, 157
camomile:
 as insect repellent, 154; as tea, 142, 154
candy:
 borage flowers, 144; mint leaves, 144; rose petals, 144; violet blossoms, 144

207

cyclamen, germination of, 12

daisies, planting of, 9
dandelion(s), 74-75
    as coffee substitute, 141; medical
    use of, 160; wine, 142
decorations, plants used as, 152-54
dibble, 14
dill, 116
    as flavoring, 116
dolls, corncob, 151

earth almond. *See* Chufa
earthworms, 39
earwigs, 39-40
eggplants, 75-76, 186
eggshells:
    as cutworm pesticide, 38; as ferti-
    lizer, 24; seeding in, 12, 16
elder:
    as aphid pesticide, 34; as maggot
    pesticide, 42; as mole repellent, 48
electric cables, for hotbeds, 6
endive, 76-77
    winter storage of, 130
escarole. See Endive
eschalots. *See* Shallots
Eucharis, miticide for, 44
evergreens, as mulch, 181

fencing, early advice on, 5
fennel, 116
    as flavoring 116
fenugreek, 116-17
    as flavoring, 116; sprouts, 117
ferns, scale control for, 49
fertilizers, 19-31
    ammonia, 20; ashes, 20-21; bones,
    21; burned earth, 21-22; castor
    beans, 22; coffee grounds, 22; egg-
    shells, 24; fish, 24; greensand, 24;
    hair, 24-25; hooves, 25; leather,
    25; liquid compost, 31; manure,
    26; manure water, 31; mud, 26;
    oils, 28; rags, 28; salt, 28; salt-
    peter, 29; sawdust, 29; seaweed,
    29-30; soluble, 30-31; soot tea,
    31; *See also* Compost; Mulch; in-
    dividual flowers and vegetables
fetticus. *See* Corn salad
finohio. *See* Florence fennel
fish:
    as fertilizer, 24; majoram used to

catch, 118; as mole repellent, 48
flea beetles, 40
flies, 40
Florence fennel, 77-78
flowers, 167-91
    arranging plants in beds, 178-180;
    cuttings, 180; frost protection for,
    181-82; perennials, 186; planters,
    186-87; planting of, 9-10; pot-
    ting, 187-88; pressed, 153-54; *See
    also* individual listings
fluoride, as cause of plant damage, 18
foxglove, medical use of 156
fragrance, plants used as, 151-52
Franklin, Benjamin, 145
French endive. *See* Chicory
French spinach. *See* Orach
fruit trees:
    ant pesticide for, 34; bark insect
    pesticides for, 35; fertilizer for, 20;
    new varieties of, 199-200; soap as
    pesticide for, 44-45
fruit waters, 143
fuchsias, 169-70

garden almond. *See* Chufa
garden cress. *See* Cress
garden etiquette, 182
gardenias, 24
gardening, new developments in, 192-
    201
gardenless garden, 182-83
garden rocket. *See* Rocket
garlic, 78
    medical use of, 162; winter stor-
    age of, 130, 132
gentians, germination of, 12
gladiolas, 170-71
glauconite, as fertilizer, 24
globe artichoke, 54, 155
gooseberries, 78
gourds, 145-48
green fly. *See* Aphids
greensand, as fertilizer, 24
ground cherry, 79
grubs, 41

hair, as fertilizer, 24-25
hand cream recipe, 5
· hanging baskets, 183
hawthorn hedges, 5
head crops, rotation of, 10
hellebore, 36, 43, 49

lungwort, 156

maggots, 41-43
magnetism, and growing experiments, 8-9
mango melon. *See* Vine peach
manure:
    in crop rotation, 11; as fertilizer, 26; green, 11; for hotbeds, 7; as mulch, 10
manure water, as fertilizer, 31
marjoram, 118
    to catch fish, 118; as cleaner, 144; as flavoring, 118; medical use of, 162-63; vinegar, 165; winter storage of, 130
martynia, 84, 152
mattocks, 15
mealy bugs, 43
medicines, plants used as, 155-65
    balm, 156; balsam apple, 158; calendula, 158; canna, 158-59; catnip, 159; celery, 160; chervil, 160; chicory, 160; comfrey, 160; dandelion, 160; garlic, 162; horehound, 162; hyssop, 162; lavender, 162; marjoram, 162-63; mint, 163; onions, 163; rhubarb, 163; rose, 163; rosemary, 163-64; sage, 164; savory, 164; sesame, 164; soapwort, 164; tansy, 165; thyme, 165; tobacco, 165; tomato, 165
melons:
    cantaloupes, 61-62; citron, 70; pomegranate, 151-52; Queen Anne's pocket, 151-52; rotation of, 10; soot as pesticide for, 44; watermelons, 110-11
mercury, 36
mignonette, 173
mildew, 43
mint geranium. *See* Costmary
mints, 118-119
    as flavorings, 118-19; leaf candy, 144; medical use of, 163 as teas, 142; winter storage of, 130; *See also* individual listings
mirliton. *See* Chayote
mites, 44, 49
moles, 47-48
moon, influence of, 9-10

mountain spinach. *See* Orach
mud, as fertilizer, 26
mulch, 10
    evergreens as, 181; grubs in, 41; for potatoes, 10; trash, 42; *See also* Compost; Fertilizer; individual flowers and vegetables
muskmelon. *See* Cantaloupe
mustard, 85
    as maggot pesticide, 43

nasturtiums, 85-86
    germination of, 12
New Zealand spinach, 86
nitrogen, in fertilizer, 19

oak bark, as aphid pesticide, 34
oils:
    as fertilizer, 28; as maggot pesticide, 42
okra, 87
    as coffee substitute, 141; winter storage of, 131
onions, 87, 89
    fertilizer for, 20; medical use of, 163; rotation of, 11; winter storage of, 132
orach, 89-90
oregano, 162
oven drying, 125-26
oystr shells, as clubroot preventive, 38

pansies, 174
Paris green, 48-49
Park, William J., 198
Parnham, Harold J., 194
parsley, 119-20
    as flavoring, 119-20; winter storage of, 130
parsnips, 89-90
    rotation of, 10; winter storage of, 132
peach water, 143
peanuts, 90
pear water, 143
peas, 90-91
    rotation of, 10, 11
peat blocks, transplanting with, 16
    pennyroyal, 154; medical use of, 156
pepone. *See* Cantaloupe
pepper(s), 91-92

as fly repellent, 40; as insect repellent for roses, 46; winter storage of, 132

peppergrass. *See* Cress

peppermint, 118-19
drying of, 130; as tea, 142

perlite, fluorine in, 18

pest control, 32-51
See also individual pests

pesticides, old-fashioned, 44-47

petunias, planting of, 9

phosphorus, in fertilizer, 19

pickles and preserves, 126
citron, 70; cucumber, 74; vine peach, 109

ploughs, 15

pomander, plant used as, 151-52

pomegranate melon, 151-52

pompion. *See* Cantaloupe

potash:
to control ants, 32; in fertilizer, 19

potassium sulfide. *See* Sulfide of potassium

potato(es), 92-93
fertilizer for, 20, 26, 28, 93-94; mulching of, 10; planting of, 9; rotation of, 11; scab in, 20; water, as earthworm pesticide, 39; winter storage of, 133

potato bugs, 48-49, 76

pot marigold. *See* Calendula

potpourri, recipe for, 152

pumpkins, 102-3
winter storage of, 133

Queen Anne's pocket melon, 151-52

radishes, 94
winter storager of, 133

rags, as fertilizer, 28

rakes, 15

raspberry(ies), 94-95
new varieties of, 200; water, 143

red spiders, 49

Relyea, Kenneth E., 198

rhubarb, 95-96
medical use of, 163; winter storage of, 133-34

rocket, 96

rocket salad. *See* Rocket

rock weed, as webworm repellent, 36-37

Rodale, Robert, *Organic Gardening and Farming*, 195-96

root aphids, 35

root crops:
planting of, 10; rotation of, 10; *See also* individual listings

roquette. *See* Rocket

rose(s):
caterpillar pesticide for, 36; Christmas, 12, 36; conserve, 163; fertilizer for, 31; indoor growing of, 174, 176; mealy bug pesticide for, 43; medical use of, 163; oil of, 149; petal beads, 155; petal candy, 144; plastic spray for, 182; in potpourri, 152; red pepper as insect pellent for, 46; scale pesticide for, 49; vinegar of, 163; water, 149

rosemary, 120
as flavoring, 120; as insect repellent, 154; medical use of, 163-64; winter storage of, 130

rucola. *See* Rocket

rue, 154

rutabaga(s), 96-97, 109
winter storage of, 136

rye, rotation of, 11

saffron, substitute for, 114

sage, 121
as flavoring, 121; as insect repellent, 154; medical use of, 164; as tobacco substitute, 151

salsify, 97
winter storage of, 134

sal soda, as bark insect pesticide, 35

salt:
as cutworm pesticide, 38; on developing fruits, 36; as fertilizer, 26, 28-29; as maggot peticide, 41; as slug and snail pesticide, 50; as weed killer, 28, 29

saltpeter:
as clubroot preventive, 38; as fertilizer, 29

savory, summer, 121
as flavoring, 121; medical use of, 164

savory, winter, 121
as flavoring, 121; medical use of, 164